My Saviour

Rita Giddings

III Clink
Street

Published by Clink Street Publishing 2022

Copyright © 2022

First edition.

ISBN:
978-1-914498-19-0 - paperback
978-1-914498-20-6 - ebook

*I dedicate this book to my Mother, who encouraged me in so many ways,
who I love and miss very much, may she rest in peace.*

***

The names of some locations and people within this book have been changed

***

*My faith has helped me through many difficulties and given me hope, peace and joy.
I hope that by reading this book that you may also come to know the blessings that our Saviour Jesus Christ can give to you.*

.

FORWARD

By Father Matthew Pittam

I am glad to be writing this forward for Rita Giddings. Her book is very brave indeed, as it presents to the world the depths of her heart. We are invited to be witnesses of Rita's journey through life and her walk with God who is ever present as part of this rich and diverse tapestry. What impresses me most about this story is the fact that it does not shy away from the reality that following God can be tough as we face all that the world presents to us. Rita is presented with many trials and tribulations, which would test the faith of many of us, and yet, for her, it enables reflection upon how God sustains her through challenges.

This book could be a great help and aid to those who face a route through life, which is demanding and fraught with setbacks and disappointments. This is especially true as Rita is seen to pick herself up and continue her journey with her faith in God strengthened. There is no trite explanation for the suffering that she experiences but rather an honest and deep reflection on how she has coped with the aid of the gift of faith.

Rita's story is not one of sadness though. I found despite the difficult issues that this story unfolds, a great and resounding theme of joy and peace. In that sense, it becomes a gentle reflection, which remains accessible to many readers who will surely benefit from the honesty and integrity found in these pages.

Rita is very candid about her relationship with her father. She demonstrates a great love for him, whilst at the same time presenting him as a challenging character on many levels. In today's world, people often struggle with the concept of 'God the Father' because of what is lacking in their own earthly parental relationships. This has led a significant number of people to have doubts or dismiss the possibility of having a loving father. This is not so for Rita who seems to have developed a far more profound relationship with God directly as a consequence of her life experience.

*If I were to sum up this book theologically then I would
look no further than the words of the Psalmist,
Lord, you have examined me and you know me.
You know everything I do;
From far away you understand all my thoughts.
You see me, whether I am working or resting;
You know all my actions.
Even before I speak,
You already know what I will say.
You are all around me on every side;
You protect me with your power.
Your knowledge of me is too deep;
It is beyond my understanding.
Where could I go to escape from you?
Where could I get away from your presence?
If I went up to heaven, you would be there;
If I lay down in the world of the dead, you would be there;
If I flew away beyond the east
or lived in the furthest part of the west,
You would be there to lead me.
You would be there to help me."*

– Psalm 139 Good News Bible

CHAPTER 1

My childhood and a miraculous experience

I was looking after my parents' bungalow as they were on holiday. It was late summer, a warm cloudy day and the apple tree, which was loaded with eating apples was swaying about in the breeze. Just before the holiday, my father who was a very controlling person, had a difference of opinion with me over my adult children and was angry with me because I did not agree with him. As I was watering the geraniums and tidying up in the kitchen, I bent down to put away some dishes in the cupboard. I gasped with shock as suddenly my back felt as if a knife had been stabbed through it. The pain was horrendous. It took me a while to stand up again and with great difficulty, limp back to the car and return home. I am usually very busy and would not think of going to bed unless I felt really rough but I was laid up for a week with excruciating spasms. When I prayed for an answer as to why I was experiencing this and what on earth I had done, the Lord brought back to me the resentfulness that my father had towards me just before he and my mother went away on holiday. It seemed as though He was telling me that my father had inflicted this torment on me as a punishment. I wondered how this could be possible and continued to pray for an answer. The answer came back that my father was practising witchcraft. I paused for a moment thinking back to my childhood.

When I was a small child, I went to Sunday School each week to the Methodist Chapel in the peaceful little village where we lived. Through this experience, I can remember looking up at the sky one sunny afternoon and being aware, that God was there. Often at night time though, I was fearful about going to bed unless the light was left on, because I had seen strange dark shadowy images lurking in my bedroom. I used to pull the covers right over my head before I felt safe to go to sleep. When I told my Mother, she thought I was imagining things.

On my first day of school, I was energetically running in the playground with some friends and a boy appeared from nowhere and collided with me. I suffered a black eye and had to have a week off school. This was not a very good start and I was upset when I had to go back, but within a couple of months I was enjoying being at school. An older friend whose house was right next to the railway line had taught me to draw trains and as my favourite lesson was drawing and painting they were often the subject of my work.

It was about this time that I had to have my tonsils removed. I was quite anxious about the operation and wondered what was going to happen. I had many nightmares beforehand and was glad when it was over. I remember the kind doctor who said that I was well enough to go home from hospital and what a nice bright cheerful colour my yellow cardigan was that my mum had knitted me.

When I had been at school about two years my teachers moved me up into the next class, as they seemed to think that I was doing very well. I can remember dancing with my friends round the maypole on May Day at school and there was quite a celebration. It was a lovely time of year with all the spring flowers and blossom on the trees.

I felt much more relaxed and comfortable when I was just with my mum because my father was very strict. My mum seemed to be afraid of him and he was treated with respect in our house, as he was quite intimidating. Sometimes there were rows and when he shouted, it sent shivers of fear through me.

My godmother sent me a large colourful book about animals for my birthday. I opened the parcel before I went to school and because I could not bear to leave it at home all day and wanted to look at it. I took it to school to show it to my friends. My mum tried to tell me it was not a good idea in case it was taken. Unfortunately, I did not listen and sure enough it disappeared and I never saw it again. I was heartbroken.

Just before my eighth birthday, we moved from our little cottage in a small friendly village, with its outside toilet and tin bath in front of the fire, to a bungalow that my father had designed and had built in the village where he had grown up. We had a bathroom, which was a luxury. My parents gave me a piano for my birthday and I started to have lessons to play it. I thoroughly enjoyed this and had an encouraging teacher.

My father bought me a little tent and used to put it up on the back lawn. I would sleep in it sometimes during the warm summer nights. As soon as I attended my new school, I was taught by a teacher who had taught my father. I had enjoyed my previous school so much, but here I found that the work was a year behind what I had already covered. I became bored and started to lose interest. I failed my eleven-plus exam and moved up to a comprehensive secondary school where there were grammar and lower stream classes for each year. I was placed in the upper stream of the non-grammar class.

I soon made many friends. I started learning French and really enjoyed school and although I did not struggle with my work and seemed to be getting on well, two weeks later I was transferred to the lowest class in the school. I was quite upset. No reason was given. The teacher in this class took great delight in telling all the pupils that they were the lowest of the low and there was no class in the school lower than ours. This annoyed me and made me determined to do well and prove this teacher wrong. I worked very hard and she never had any reason to complain about me. I especially enjoyed English, art and music classes. I loved writing stories and my art and music teachers were very encouraging and used to praise my work.

At the back of our new home, I could wander through about five meadows, full of buttercups and a little wood at the side of the property undisturbed where Rosebay Willow-herb flowers grew as tall as me. Often horses were put in the field at the back of our home. They used to lean over the fence and eat the peas that they could reach, that my father was growing. He was not too happy about this.

As I arrived home from school one day, I could see that my mother was upset. She told me that she had received some sad news about her brother Alan, who had been diagnosed with stomach cancer. This saddened me because like my mother my uncle was a very kind person, and was a talented artist who shared my love of drawing horses. The family were due to move house so during the summer holidays my mother and I decorated their new home, as my uncle was in hospital and my auntie was busy looking after their three children. When we learnt that the hospital could do no more to help him and he had been sent home we were devastated. I regularly attended the little Methodist Chapel in the village where we lived and I prayed for him to recover. He passed on some months later and we were all deeply saddened.

I enjoyed going to the local riding school every Saturday. I had such fun there and often helped with grooming and tacking up the ponies. My favourite steed was Golden Sovereign, a beautiful chestnut gelding with cream mane and tail. There were some lovely leafy lanes to ride along and fields to canter through. One day I saw a hare racing along in front of us. If help was needed with the sheep shearing, I used to volunteer. I watched the blacksmith shoeing the ponies and was fascinated at how he used red hot shoes, which burnt into the outer part of the ponies' hooves before nailing them into position, all of which was painless to them because he knew exactly what he was doing.

I got on very well with my cousin Tina who lived nearby and was a year older than I. She was a good friend and always full of fun. I knew that she had been suffering from meningitis and had to stay in a nearby isolation hospital, but thankfully, she seemed to recover. Then without any warning, we received the sad news that she had suddenly been taken ill while out with her parents and had died. I was very shocked and could not take it in. I spent some time at a friend's house over the next few days, to help take my mind off this terrible shock but it did not work. She was often on my mind.

Soon afterwards, my uncle Len my father's half-brother died suddenly from a heart attack after chasing some youths who were very unpleasant towards him. His family were very distressed. My father had fallen out with Uncle Len about four years previously. My mother and I found it difficult to understand my father's sullen moods and family feuds so we decided to go and visit the family and see if we could do something to rectify the problem, agreeing to keep secret our attempts to patch things up. Unfortunately, father had his arm twisted, when I forgot about the secret and blurted out one meal time what a nice time we had spent at their home. I've never forgotten the look on my father's face. It went from a look of annoyance to anger and then melted in a smile. Soon afterwards, he made a point of going to see his half-brother and making friends with him shortly before he suddenly died.

One cold frosty November evening my father seemed particularly depressed. He spoke of his mother who had apparently abandoned him and his sibling when he was thirteen years old. He said that he wondered where she was now. I could not help but feel sorry for him. I could only wonder at the sad upbringing that he must have experienced, but always refused to talk about like a carefully guarded secret. This was the only time he ever spoke about her.

As a family, we went away each year for a break. I remember the very rough Channel crossing to Guernsey when my mother and I realised that we were not good sailors, but once we arrived the breath taking views and lovely warm weather made it a holiday to remember. We invited a great aunt with us when we toured Scotland. The mountainous landscape was adorned with purple heather cascading down into tranquil lochs, an area of outstanding natural beauty. Some of the roads were very steep and full of dangerous bends, which were probably more suited to mountain goats than our old Rover vehicle. Each time we went away somehow the time was marred with my father going into a mood, which often lasted for several days. I always enjoyed going to visit my great aunt and uncle who lived near the coast. They were such a lovely couple and my uncle had a good sense of humour. Unfortunately, this did not deter my father from going into bad moods there as well which was embarrassing for my mother and I.

The only time I felt really relaxed on holiday, was when my mother took me up to York on the train to stay with my godmother. It was such a serene and happy place to be. I listened to many interesting stories of older relatives who I had not had the opportunity of meeting. York was such a lovely city to wander around. I enjoyed searching for souvenirs in the shops. It was hard to go back home afterwards as the atmosphere was completely different in our own home.

When I reached the age of thirteen, I suddenly decided that I did not want to go to church anymore. I felt it was boring and I told my parents so that they would not expect me to go anymore.

Unexpectedly my father encouraged me to continue attending, which I thought at the time was very odd as he never came to church with us. I eventually decided to continue helping at the Sunday School and went to evening services with my mother.

A few months later, the Methodist minister visited me at our home and asked me if I would like to make a commitment as a Christian and become a Church Member. I said that I would think about this, as I really was not sure at the time.

During the year that followed, I continued to attend the Sunday afternoon meetings for young people at our church. At each session, we were split into groups of about six and several youth leaders led us in a time of reflection of Christ's love for us. One Sunday our leader, a man, in his forties, with a deep Christian faith, told us to imagine that we were living during the time of the Second World War, that we were Jewish and the Nazis had captured us. Jesus came along and volunteered to take our place as we were led to the gas chamber and now we were free to go. This picture had a great impact upon me and for the first time, I really believed that Jesus had died for me to save me from my sins. I now came to know Jesus as a friend and made a decision that I wanted to become a Church Member. Several of my friends also joined me in this. There were about six of us who went along to the weekly meetings for preparation. When I was fifteen, I attended the service for new members along with my friends. It was a joyful time. The church was packed with all age groups who had come to support us. We received a lot of encouragement from all the members of the church.

Surprisingly I now had the opportunity to transfer back to the class at school that, years previously I was mysteriously removed from. While all of my friends were leaving school at fifteen, I was given the opportunity to stay on and take exams.

My father was a very strict person. He expected me always to do well at school or I would receive a stern lecture from him. He was so strict that he would not allow my mother to speak when we were visiting relatives and expected her to stay quiet. Every couple of months he would go into sulks for two or three days, when he stayed silent and sour faced. Nothing and no one could talk him out of it. He frightened me when he was like this because we never knew what he would do next.

Although I enjoyed most of the subjects that I was studying at school, I did struggle with maths and in particular algebra. My father decided that he would help me with this. His way of showing me seemed completely different to that of the teacher's and so I felt more confused than I had to begin with. I started to feel that I was quite hopeless at maths and that perhaps I never would be any good at this subject.

I found it difficult to speak to my dad. If I needed to talk to him about anything important, I often could not bring myself to raise the subject and used to put it off sometimes for days. I tried but I found it increasingly more difficult to communicate with my father. I even found it difficult to talk to my mother quite often. I was an only child. My sister had sadly been stillborn five years previously. My cat was good company for me at home and I used to spend lots of time playing with her and reading. I also loved to listen to music especially The Beatles and many other groups of the early sixties. My father objected to this and most of my record playing was done when he was out.

My father had no sense of humour and was usually serious. Occasionally though my cousins, auntie and uncle from Lancashire used to shake us out of the doldrums when they visited us. We had a lot of fun during these times. My uncle and eldest cousin both had a really good sense of humour and I had a lot in common with my cousin Mary. I could really let my hair down and have a laugh without my father complaining, although my auntie who was my father's sister seemed quite serious as well, but she was very kind.On one occasion, I was able to sit and talk to my father after watching the evening news while my mother was preparing supper. We spoke about people who have done wrong in this world but do not seem to receive any punishment for their misdeeds. I said to him that I believe that our Heavenly Father knows all the things that people do wrong and will deal with them either here or in the next life. He then said something that puzzled me "You don't want to know what I have been doing" in a mischievous voice. I did not like the sound of this but felt that I should not question him any further at that time.

During my final year, I missed all my friends that had left school. Many of the girls in my present class were arrogant troublemakers and some of them mysteriously developed a bad attitude towards me and started to bully me. I could often hear them talking about me behind my back which was hurtful, although I had done nothing to upset them. I am sure that because I was encouraged to wear old-fashioned clothes especially by my father this must have given them some fuel for this bad behaviour. As the ridicule and bullying continued, I developed an inferiority complex. The main friend who I had in this class, and who I had spoken about to my parents suddenly turned her back on me and found other friends to mix with. My father had strongly disapproved of her previously with no apparent reason. He had not even met her. I was determined to throw myself into my work, which I did, and I worked even harder. I felt very alone and troubled, with no one to turn to.

My mother wanted to learn to drive so my father said he would take her out and teach her. Perhaps my father thought I could not be trusted at home on my own, but I was expected to go along as well, which seemed very unfair on my mum. My father was very unpleasant towards my mum, which caused her to be nervous and make mistakes. I felt very sorry for her. She decided that she did not want to continue to learn to drive because she felt so demoralised with the brutal bullying she was receiving from my father. I do not think that she could afford to have lessons at a driving school, or I am sure that this is what she would have done.

At church the next Sunday, I was invited to go on a retreat for a week, to a coastal town in Norfolk. Unfortunately, my parents both put their names down to go as well and as my father seemed so controlling, I thought that this would spoil my freedom to have a laugh with friends and relax. I felt undermined and untrusted by my parents as I was now sixteen years old.

My exams were now over and I left school after the summer term elated, because I no longer had to face the bullies. I can remember singing 'School's Out' by Alice Cooper.

A week later, I was stepping aboard the coach for the holiday at the coast. Several other families travelled with us, but mostly younger children. During that week, something wonderful happened to me. I woke up one morning and felt so totally relaxed and at peace and worry free and as though a big load had been lifted from my shoulders. My hands that had been shaking with nerves were no longer shaking and the gut-wrenching misery that I had felt had left me. I did not understand at the time but I had been baptised in the Holy Spirit and filled with the peace that passes all understanding.

When I returned home, I can remember walking down to the local corner shop to buy a choc-ice but when I went to pay for it the shopkeeper said, "What has happened, you have changed." I told her that I had been away on a lovely holiday and was amazed that she recognised the transformation in me.

My mother's friend embarrassed me, only a few weeks before, when she said, "How is Rita going to manage at college in September?" She had apparently understood my nervous introvert behaviour, which seemed to have escaped my parents. This situation had now been wonderfully reversed as God had radically changed me into a happy and confident person, who enjoyed life! I felt like a new person and found that I could be more outgoing and could mix with all sorts of people. My clothes sense seemed more important to me and I refused to wear anything remotely old-fashioned any more. I joined a local organisation made up of young people, which met weekly and was led by a young man who had a good sense of humour. Every time I went there, I laughed a lot which was just what I needed. We got involved in all sorts of voluntary work, which included, decorating the inside of a building, which was to be used for charity work. We exchanged jokes as we worked and it was a lovely, light hearted atmosphere. Part of the work that we were encouraged to do was to choose an elderly person and offer to visit them weekly to help out with their garden or do their shopping.

I approached an elderly neighbour, who was really thankful for the help I offered. It helped me as well because I found gardening very therapeutic. At about this time I found an interesting book to read written by a Methodist minister about psychology and as I read this book, I started to recognise the tricks my unconscious mind had been playing on me causing me to become introvert and suffer with an inferiority complex. After my healing and baptism in the Holy Spirit, my life was completely changing for the better. I praised Jesus, as He is a wonderful Friend to me.

We organised a charity concert at our local town theatre and each of us got involved either on the stage or behind the scenes. I practised some music that was in the charts to play on the piano. Some of my fellow musicians, although very talented, were so nervous that they lost their voices. I do not think that I went on to the stage in my own strength. I saw what looked like hundreds of people looking up at me from the audience. I sat down, but I do not remember feeling nervous. I had practiced the music so well that it was just automatic. I successfully completed my performance to a good applause. The Lord was really looking after me.

A few weeks later, I received the results of my exams. I had passed them all apart from one 'O' level music! Never mind there would be other opportunities I was sure. I was elated that I had passed all the other seven subjects and praised God because I knew that He had been with me through each exam paper that I had sat.

CHAPTER 2

Saving up for my passion – a horse

September arrived and I started my Secretarial course at the local College. I found it so easy to make friends, and I do not think that there was one person in my class that I did not get on well with as we all had a lot in common. We worked, but we were able to have some fun as well as it was a more relaxed atmosphere than at school.

I joined a young people's Christian ecumenical group, which I really enjoyed as I made many friends here as well as the other club I attended. This organisation got involved in all sorts of interesting projects. We did a house-to-house survey to show the feasibility of a new church on a brand-new estate which was in the process of being built. We also did a twenty-five-mile sponsored walk to raise money for local charities.

There was a Christmas party at the college and I met and danced with my first boyfriend to Beach Boys music. I could not believe how my life had changed and how I was getting so much out of life now with all my friends. I was so thankful for what God was doing for me.

Our church had a problem with the roof and there was a need to raise money to repair it. I used to attend church meetings held to maintain and plan new ideas for our church. I suggested that we hold a summer fete to raise money for the repairs needed, but I had little support with this idea. People in the meeting said, who will organise it? I told them that I would if they all did something to help. Amazingly, they all agreed to this. I felt that Jesus was really with me in this and I received so much enjoyment out of doing this work. We had all sorts of stalls. I myself had a disco stall where people could choose the music they wanted to listen to. I tried to get someone well known to open it as I thought this would draw people in so I contacted a local pop group who had recently had a record in the charts, but they were too busy. I asked the mayor instead and advertised it in the local paper. I was surprised when the press came and took photos! It was a successful event and we raised a third of the money for the work that needed to be done on the roof. Over the next two summers, I organised the same event until we had enough money to repair the roof. I also organised Christmas parties for our church congregation, which I thoroughly enjoyed. I really felt that the Lord was leading me in this and we had such good fun at the parties. It was a lovely atmosphere.

After finishing college I looked for my first job and after several interviews I set my heart on a

Receptionist/shorthand typist job at a company which produced power station manuals, and I was told due to the secrecy of the work there, I would have to sign the Official Secrets Act. I can remember telling my parents about this. It sounded as though I had the job but I never heard anything more from them. Then my father organised a job for me in the typing pool at the same company where he worked.

I was very unhappy because it was like going back to school as I was repeating everything I had learnt at college. It seemed so futile. At the end of the first week the manager of the publishing company called at our home and asked to speak to me. He asked me if I wanted the job we had spoken about and I said that I was very interested. He explained that he had sent me a letter inviting me to start the job, and as I had obviously not received it, he assumed that it must have got lost in the post. I was so relieved and could not wait to start working there after giving a week's notice at the depressing typing pool. The staff at my new job were all very jovial and put me at my ease and even the manager seemed very kind. I worked with the secretary who I got on well with. On Fridays, it was my job to go and buy cream cakes for everyone to go with their afternoon tea. Every time I walked into the illustrator's office they made me laugh with their jokes. The authors were so kind and helpful. I enjoyed my job so much that I did not want to have a holiday!

My father planned a holiday to Anglesey, without consulting me, for my mother, him and myself. He even invited my grandparents to come along as well. I cringed at the thought because at the age of seventeen I did not want to go on holiday with my parents or my grandparents, although I thought a lot of them. I made it quite clear how I felt to no avail. When we arrived, I just wanted to go off and do my own thing so I took a sketching pad and recorded parts of the coastline. This annoyed my father immensely. My mother told him to leave me alone as she had much more compassion and understanding, but was often afraid to show this in front of my father, and when my grandparents agreed with her, this enraged my father even more. Within a couple of days of this tug of war situation on holiday he went into a huge sulk which lasted several days, and ending in my grandparents who no longer felt welcome going home on the train. We returned home early and it was not early enough for me! I did sympathise with my mum the way my dad bossed her about and sometimes tried to stick up for her. Unfortunately, my father could also become violent towards her, but while I was at home, I made sure that I would not let him harm her.

I started learning to drive and had a good instructor who was very kind and patient. I did not earn much money and could only afford to learn in a Mini, which was the most reasonably priced lessons available at that time. My father took me out to practice in our Rover 80 which was a large car with no power steering and this was quite a contrast between the two cars, but I managed to progress even though his patience was a little frayed at times. The day came for my driving test when I felt reasonably confident but a little nervous. Amazingly, I seemed to come through the test with ease. However, I had a shock when the examiner told me that I had failed my driving test because I was too far over on my right-hand turn. I was very surprised because I thought I had driven well that day. I returned to work very disappointed and said that I would not bother to take the test again.

At work, everyone rallied round and told me to take the test again and to book it right away. They made me laugh and told me that because I was a young woman the instructor was nervous about passing me the first time!

During the second driving test, I took, this time I was very nervous. I made some quite bad mistakes. It was a different examiner. He seemed kind and understanding and he passed me. I could not believe it, but I was delighted.

After I had passed my test, my father allowed me to borrow the car, on my own, which was a real surprise. I drove over to a new riding school about ten miles away and booked in to ride there on Sunday afternoons. The horses were very classy and had impeccable manners. I felt safe here as the horses were so well schooled. They did not put a foot wrong. I went out for hacks in the beautiful surrounding countryside and nearby villages with a group of others and the instructor leading us.

As I progressed and became more confident, I was introduced to their cross-country course, which I had a lot of fun with. One horse that I rode was a large black hunter, he was lovely but he did not like water or jumping over obstacles where he could not see where he was going to land on the other side! As we cantered up to a small water jump one day, he ground to a halt, snorting and looking down at it in horror. When I encouraged him to go on, he took a giant cat leap over the water as though it was about six foot wide. We must have looked very funny.

Another day I was given a beautiful grey horse to ride. The grey horse was a talented showjumper and leapt about two foot higher than necessary at every obstacle. He was so graceful and it was such a wonderful experience as we took all the fences in the show jumping course.

I longed to have my own horse and at about that time a new instructor who was an ex-jockey came to the riding school. He was keen himself to buy a retired racehorse and influenced me to think the same way, which was a big mistake.

Eventually the riding school manager and two of the instructors and myself attended a racehorse sale. On the low wage that I earned compared to my male counterparts I struggled to save up to buy a horse. Foolishly, I asked my parents to lend me some money promising to pay them back. My father gave me £80 to buy a horse but I knew that this would not be enough money to buy a healthy horse. I was warned by the riding school manager not to make a mistake and bid for an unsuitable horse but unfortunately, temptation got the better of me. We watched with interest as one by one, the horses were led into the ring and auctioned. My heart ruled my head and I found myself against the advice of the riding school manager bidding for a beautiful bay thoroughbred gelding. I just had enough money to pay for him and we brought him back to the riding school.

My father was furious that I had bought a horse. I think that he thought he had not given me enough money to buy anything at the sale. He appeared worried about my safety and grudgingly took me to buy a second-hand bridle and saddle.

I searched without success for a field for him to graze in near to where I lived, but was repeatedly turned down by farmer after farmer. Eventually a field was offered to me, along with a stable. Cosmopolitan was a graceful well-mannered horse. I had no worries about him taking off with me at full gallop. He and I got on very well. Unfortunately, his field was marshy which caused problems with his feet. He developed thrush due to the damp conditions and also became lame from a previous racing injury, which had affected the tendons on his lower legs. I was very upset. The vets that came out to examine him could offer no real help but gave me a large bill that I could not afford to pay.

I was devastated and started to come out in a severe dermatitis rash on both arms with the worry of everything. I wrote to the vets telling them how disappointed I was that they could not do anything to help my horse's lameness and that I found the bill extortionate. Thankfully, they reduced the bill by two thirds, which was a relief and I was able to pay it. I kept the horse for three months and stabled him over the winter mucking him out daily. The riding school manager offered to have Cosmo for a year and just put him out to grass to see if his tendons improved. I made a decision, which I now know was wrong. I returned him to the racecourse sales and sold him to a farmer in the south of England who said he was going to allow him to rest for some time before trying to ride him. I always regret selling him.

Eventually due to expansion of the company where I worked, the secretary and I were given a tiny office to share, without any daylight. We both found these working conditions difficult to work in so I looked for another job and hoped to combine this with a pay rise.

My new career change was as a shorthand typist at a solicitor's office. I had not been able to keep my shorthand speeds up in my previous position, so as I struggled so much on the first day, I decided to buy myself a new shorthand book on the way home, and spent the rest of that week studying and practicing to achieve a good speed, which gave me more confidence. I did not realise how depressing this job was going to be as it was working in the probate department sorting out the wills of deceased people, but I still managed to get some enjoyment out of my working day by making friends with the other typists in my office. At Christmas time, we had a laugh when one of us suggested what a good idea it would be to sing some carols over the intercom. Afterwards we found out that one of the solicitors was in his office eating his lunch. Woops! That same lunchbreak after we had all had our lunch, a mince pie and a glass of sherry given to all the staff, I can remember saying to my colleagues wouldn't it be good to liven our town up a bit as nothing very interesting happens here. We went into the centre of town and I rode round the clocktower roundabout three times on my bike. All the traffic stopped!

At this point, I was looking for more of a social life and joined the eighteen-plus group. I met many new friends here. There was always something interesting to do. We went on outings and had exciting activities like go-kart racing and homemade log raft races. We had discos and dances and had a great time. By this time, several young men were asking me out for dates but I was selective and preferred to be single, have a good laugh and mix with a variety of people.

I made up my mind that I was going to save up for another horse. As I received such a low wage and I was giving my parents a responsible amount of board each week I could no longer afford to go out and so spent a lot of time at home. I saved up enough money to buy a horse. However, after nearly a year my mother repeatedly urged me to start going out and mixing with people again as I was becoming quiet and withdrawn.

Eventually I moved on to another job where I became a secretary and received another pay rise. At this place, I was sitting in a large office and wondered how I would get on with everyone. I soon found out that they were a great bunch of people. Besides working hard for my boss who was a very pleasant person, we had paperclip fights across the office and plenty of jokes were exchanged.

The sales manager was always making promises that he could not keep with delivery schedules. On April Fool's Day, I decided to have some fun at my boss and the sales manager's expense. I typed up a telex message, which looked as though it was incoming from one of the company's well-known customers, describing a part that was very urgent. The telex also stated that they were coming down by helicopter to collect it and to please advise a suitable landing site. I took this in to my boss's office trying to keep a straight face. As I was walking out, he read it and called to his sales colleague in the next office with some urgency. They both read it. Then things started to get out of hand, as they both called the general manager to read this message. At that point, I thought I had better say something, so I crept into the office and said April Fool. They all fell about laughing which was just as well as the general manager did not have much of a sense of humour.

My dad used to become wound up about bad luck. He was quite superstitious. He became upset if he accidentally spilled salt and would throw a pinch of it over his shoulder. If a mirror got broken and I can only remember this happening once, he woefully informed us that it would bring seven years bad luck. He insisted that an umbrella, was never opened up in the house. My mother and I listened to this and believed it because he was so serious and stern about it. He also could be over-possessive, resentful and sometimes manipulative about me going out and enjoying friends' company.

Several of my friends asked me if I would like to go on holiday with them to Italy. I said that I would have to think it over as I had spent some time saving up for a horse and it would take all the money I had saved.

After a long painful decision, I decided to go on holiday with my friends. It made my decision more difficult, because I had recently been offered a beautiful grey mare by the manager at the riding school. I eventually decided against buying her because she seemed too placid.

Our outward flight to Italy was bumpy as we hit turbulence. We had flown into a thunderstorm over the Dolomite Mountains.

The air hostess and many of the passengers looked alarmed. I just hoped that everything would be all right and I felt no fear as I prayed about the situation.

The heat engulfed us as we landed safely at our destination and were taken by coach to our hotel. We stayed at a friendly family run hotel. Each day we sunbathed on the beach and ran into the sea to swim because the water was so warm, completely different to the cold sea in England. The home cooked meals were delicious and very generous. As we were wandering around the town, we discovered several nightclubs and bars to go to in the evenings where we could dance. We met some of the local Italians who were charming and learnt a little Italian but we stuck together as a group for protection. The Italian men were good looking, tanned and dark but very pushy. I refused to be pressurised into a serious relationship that would probably come to an end as soon as we left Italy. However, there was one of these young men that caught my eye. His name was Mario and every time I met up with him at a disco or nightclub, my heart skipped a beat. I knew that I would find it difficult to leave Italy at the end of our holiday. He and his friend took us to Venice while we were there and we were amazed to see what a beautiful city it is. I bought a multi coloured glass vase, from the glassworks in Venice for my mum. My friends and I hired cycles, which were joined together in pairs with a sun canopy. We all thoroughly enjoyed our holiday and were sad when we had to come home.

When I returned to work a friend there asked me if I wanted her to read my cards. I had not had the Christian grounding within the Methodist church to understand how wrong this was and agreed. She proceeded to give me a brief fortune telling session through reading the playing cards that she had with her as I was feeling lonely at the time and did not have a boyfriend. What she said cheered me up for a while but I would have been far better handing over how I felt in prayer.

I used to meet up with a group of about eighteen other girls on a Friday evening and enjoy a social evening as we shared a few drinks around the town centre pubs. Drunkenness was rare in our town centre then. On a Saturday evening, I would go with a friend or group of friends to a dance where there was a band playing. Then, to finish off the weekend on Sunday I used to go horse riding and jumping. Sometimes I limped into work on the Monday if I had fallen off the day before!

My parents went away on holiday and left me to look after our home myself. I had several parties and enjoyed inviting people from different backgrounds and mixing them together! I enjoyed making the food for the parties myself. I cooked Italian food from scratch, as pizzas were not on sale in UK shops then. Making cakes and icing them in an array of colours was also something that I did because it was different.

CHAPTER 3

The Wedding

A few weeks later at work one lunchtime I found my colleagues bunched round a table with an upturned glass in the middle. They were asking it questions and it was moving. I do not know why I did it, but I asked a question, did not like the answer, said that it was rubbish and that I wanted nothing more to do with this. I thought nothing more about it and rode home on my bike for lunch.

That evening I was reading an interesting book in bed before I went to sleep. My parents were fast asleep and the house was quiet. I heard a sinister loud noise close to where I was which sounded like someone breathing. I panicked. The first thing I thought of was to pray to God and ask Him to remove whatever it was from my room. I was so relieved when the noise was quickly removed. I still felt panicky and could not sleep. I told my mum the following day and she was shocked. She told me to have nothing to do with having my fortune told as this goes against our Christian faith. She told me of when she had only just got married, went with her sister-in-law to a fair and the fortune teller had told her that her husband Alan – my mum's brother – would die when he was thirty-five. This obviously really upset them both. The frightening thing is that this really did happen. This was my Uncle Alan who died when I was twelve years old. I took this seriously especially after the experience I had just had. I turned more to my Christian faith, started reading the Bible regularly and found it very comforting.

One evening when I was out with my friends, I met a young man who reminded me of Mario who I had met on holiday. He was dark haired and tanned. I started to go out with him and soon came to realise that it was not a tan, but the colour of his skin. My father was horrified that I was going out with an Asian and tried his best to split us up. The more he tried, the more I felt like leaving home because I wanted to make my own mind up and not have it made up for me so eventually he gave me an ultimatum, finish with my boyfriend or leave home. Although my mother was very upset, because I was twenty-one years old and had grown tired of being told what to do by my father, I left home and went to live with a girlfriend in her flat. Here my boyfriend could visit me without any problems and I continued to go out with him. After we had been going out with each other for about seven months, his sister died tragically of a stomach virus and dehydration. We were both very shocked. I had already met his family and got on well with them especially with his grandmother. I had fallen in love with him and could not see any harm in the difference between our cultures although he was a Sikh. I took him to a Christian conference centre for him to learn about my religion and he was open to this and did not turn his back on it. We became closer. Then something else really tragic happened. His brother who was motorcycling over to his girlfriend's house crashed and died at the scene. Nick was devastated.

His parents seemed anxious for him to marry and he was asked to consider two arranged marriages, which he refused because he loved me. I was never sure of how tolerant his parents were towards me but we had friends who had successful mixed marriages and were very happy.

Over several more months, we started to grow apart as he became more and more unreliable and his character seemed to change. It was very painful parting but we both eventually agreed to do that. I returned to my parents' home on the understanding that they would never treat me like a child again.

After about six months, I started to go out more. I met and went out with a few boyfriends for a short while. All were a disappointment compared to Nick. I was on the rebound, but worse than that, I still loved him. The only thing that would help was to pray to the Lord for help. The more I did this the more I was able to focus on my life again and be happier.

I looked for another job and was offered a secretarial job working for an engineer, which I settled into quite well. My boss, however, turned out to be quite arrogant, and the language that he dictated to me which I recorded in shorthand, transcribed into English and typed out for him in his reports and letters seemed to be full of words that could not even be found in a technical dictionary! I am sure he used to make up his own very long words to impress his colleagues. He used to expect me to polish his desk for him as well. This was unnecessary, because the cleaners cleaned our offices very well.

I used to distribute mail to the other engineers as well who sadly also seemed ignorant as they refused to answer when I said "Good morning" to them.

The personnel manager whose office was next to mine was very ill. He came back to work but it was obvious that he should not have been there. My boss lacked understanding when I told him I was concerned about his colleague and several days later, he died. I was appalled that people in the office had shown so little compassion. We went to his funeral and his wife looked so sad. I felt really sorry for her. I was starting to feel quite disillusioned about my job and the people I was working with as I found out that another man in the office, that my mother knew was having an affair with a woman who worked near him. We did not know whether to tell his wife or not, but kept quiet. It was a difficult position to be in.

At lunchtime, I used to get my Bible out and read it. It brought me great comfort. As my boss put more and more pressure on those around him to impress all those who visited his department, I found the job more stressful and developed daily headaches. My mother was worried about this and searched the papers to help me find another job. When I arrived home one evening with yet another headache, she told me about a vacancy that she had seen in the local paper for a receptionist/secretary/animal nurse in a nearby town. I was excited at the prospect of such an interesting job and applied immediately. I was invited for an interview the following Saturday.

I was nervous as I drove along to my interview. I arrived at a beautiful manor house with an arched wall leading into the large courtyard. Mr Gordon the veterinary surgeon immediately put me at my ease. I met his wife who I would also be working for if I received the job. Straight away, I felt at home and got on with them very well. The wage that they were offering me was slightly disappointing but it was a little more than I was already receiving. The typewriter in their upstairs office above the surgery was very old so I asked them if they would like a new typewriter. I reminded myself of the private purchases that I was responsible for in my present job, enabling large staff discounts on anything we purchased. They agreed that they needed a new typewriter and said that they would be in touch soon.

A couple of days later Mr Gordon rang me with an offer of the job. I was so happy and put in an order at work before I handed in my notice for two new typewriters one for me and one for my new place of work. I managed to receive 55% discount on them both. My new employers were impressed.

I loved my new job and had three cats to keep me company in the office. They used to come and inspect everything that I was doing! I assisted in the surgery, which doubled into an operating theatre, and struggled to cope while operations were carried out at first, as I kept feeling faint. Eventually they told me that if I could not manage without feeling faint within two weeks perhaps the job was not right for me. I was relieved that more and more I was able to cope and enjoy my job.

After the operations, I washed and sterilised the instruments in a special sterilisation unit. I also made up medicines for the cows, which consisted of magnesium. Sometimes they became deficient in this mineral and would collapse. I learnt quite a lot about veterinary work there and as I loved animals so much thrived in this job.

A few months later my friend Kath rang me and invited me to go with her to a dance that evening. I had nothing arranged so I agreed to go. As we entered the dance hall, we could see that it was crowded as usual. Kath and I liked to have a laugh. Most of the other girls were dancing but there were some men standing at the back watching. So we decided to sit down and watch them just to be different. It was not long before one of them came up and asked me to dance.

He was tall, sun tanned, blonde and charming, so I agreed and stood up to dance. He disappeared! When I looked behind me, he had sat on my chair! I thought to myself that he seems to have a good sense of humour and spent the rest of the evening with him. I liked him very much and thought it was too good to be true that he would want to see me again. At the end of the evening though he asked me for my telephone number and said he would ring me. He also arranged to come over to see me.

We met up a few days later when we spent a lovely evening together and arranged another date. We started to meet twice or three times a week. It was not long before he took me to meet his family. His mother was so sweet and made me feel like a member of the family. I got on well with all his family, his sisters, younger brother and his father feeling really at ease in their home. There was no tension there, unlike my own home.

We had only known each other for about three months when Jim asked me to marry him. I could not make my mind up because I had only known him for such a short time, and said that I would think about it.

A few weeks later, he told me that he wanted an answer and would like to us to be engaged. I prayed for guidance because I did not want to make a mistake. It really felt as though the Lord was saying 'Yes, this is the right man for you,' and I knew that I loved him, which had steadily grown since the first time that I had met him. With great happiness, I said yes I would like to marry him. Importantly for me he shared my Christian faith and we both went to church together on Sundays.

He felt that he should approach my parents and talk to them about us thinking of becoming engaged, as he wanted to marry me so I took him to meet them. My mother liked him very much, and made him feel welcome but I am not sure what my father thought as he was not overfriendly towards Jim but he agreed to our engagement.

Just before Christmas, Jim took me and let me choose a beautiful sapphire and diamond engagement ring and on Christmas day, we got engaged. I was so happy.

My wedding day was supposed to be the happiest day of my life, but it was marred with problems. One of the bridesmaid's dresses did not fit her properly because my father's moodiness had prevented me from travelling to Lancashire to see her for her final fitting weeks earlier. I forgot to take the flowers for my bridesmaids and myself to have our hair decorated at the hairdressers and had to go home again and fetch them.

When I was all ready and just about to leave our home to get into the car with my father he asked me if I was sure that I was making the right decision. This threw me, as it was the last thing I expected. I was sure that what I was doing was right and told him.

When we arrived at the church, we found that Jim's family had not arrived. The photographer, a friend of Jim, made jokes that perhaps the wedding would not go ahead, which really upset me. Our car circled round several times before the minister invited us inside the church, telling us that the service would have to go ahead now even though Jim's parents and brother had not arrived. The service was lovely and I was so sad that Jim's family were not there to join in. I have never forgotten how Jim looked at me as I walked up to the altar to join him.

After we had signed the register and walked out together from the church Jim's family arrived, driven by one of his friends. There was a tearful reunion. Apparently, they had become lost and could not find the church. Jim was their eldest son and they must have been very disappointed.

At the reception a fight broke out between two people who had been drinking too much, thankfully, no one was hurt and order was soon restored. My new husband and I did not realise that we should present bouquets of flowers to our mothers until we attended another wedding some months later, which made us both feel embarrassed.

Our wedding night was marred by my health problems, which was caused by side effects from medication my doctor, had given me. Thankfully, this quickly wore off and we were able to enjoy our honeymoon.

We rented a flat in a pleasant area close to a park. We had not yet saved up for our own home and decided that we did not have to be materialistic to be happy because we were contented simply that we had each other. We were involved in running a club at our local Methodist church for children aged eight to twelve years old. We organised all sorts of activities for them and they loved coming along.

I found married life hard work as Jim did not lift a finger to help me with the work needing to be done on Saturday afternoons, as I was working full time including Saturday mornings. I had hand washing to do, as we did not have a washing machine, cleaning and cooking. He also objected to me meeting my friends and because I did not want to upset him, I accepted this at the time but this did not stop him from going out for a drink on a Saturday while I was busy.

Jim had to work a shift system, which meant that I was on my own some evenings. I felt lonely on my own during the evenings and nights when he was not there. I was shocked one evening when I found a pile of pornographic magazines under our bed and was upset because I knew that Jim had finished with several girlfriends when he met me and I now thought that perhaps he was not happy with our relationship. He seemed to think that I was making a big fuss when I mentioned how I felt, but I still felt wounded and told him that he could throw them away as I did not want them in our flat.

About eighteen months later, we decided we would like to buy our own home. Still with very little savings, we discovered that this would not be easy in the town where we were living, as we could not get the mortgage that we needed there. Eventually we were accepted a mortgage for a house, which we had chosen in the nearby city, closer to where Jim worked and not far from where his parents lived. We were excited when we opened the front door to our new home. I spent the first week organising everything, making it look like home, sewing new curtains and arranging the furnishings. I started my new job and was thankful that I now had double the salary I had been receiving in the small town where we had lived. We quickly settled down in our new environment, made new friends and joined the local Methodist church.

We regularly saw Jim's parents and family. I thoroughly enjoyed going to see them as it was always so relaxed there and we had some fun. With my mother-in-law's help, I learnt quite a few cooking techniques. They always made us feel so welcome.

Two years later, I was expecting our first child. I continued to work as a secretary up to about six weeks before the birth as I felt so well.

On the day that I started to get contraction pains I did all I could to prepare everything for Jim so that his life would be made as easy as possible while I was in hospital. After going to bed that evening it was not long before my waters broke and Jim called an ambulance. I was taken into hospital at about eleven o'clock and the contractions started to get worse. I received gas and air only as I did not want to take any other drugs in case it damaged the baby. At about three-thirty, the doctor decided that the baby was stressed and needed some help to be delivered quickly. He told Jim that he must leave the room and without any anaesthetic, he cut me to give the baby more space to pass through using forceps. Our baby daughter was born safely. It was such a relief, but after speaking to other new mothers afterwards, I did wonder if what the doctor had done was right as I was in quite a bit of pain and it took a while for it to heal. He was concerned for the baby's safety though so I am glad that he put her first. Two days later Jill our new baby turned yellow and the nurse told me that she was jaundiced. She quickly recovered from this though with some extra love and care. We were able to return home from hospital about two days later. My mother very kindly came and helped for a week which was wonderful.

She was a good baby and would only wake up once during the night for feeding. We enjoyed watching her grow and playing with her, she was such a bundle of energy. I did not feel the urge to go back to work and leave her with anyone else. I hoped that we could manage to pay the mortgage and bills on Jim's wage.

There was just one thing wrong with our new home, because our kitchen was a conservatory added to the back of the house, during the summer months the temperature would reach 37°C at the heat of the day during the summer months and during the winter was as cold as the temperature outside!

Everyone made such a fuss of Jill during her first Christmas. She was wide eyed and fascinated by the Christmas tree and all the presents. Her grandparents loved her dearly and when we went to visit Jim's parents, her grandmother gave her some ice cream to try which she enjoyed. We felt so happy that we now had our own family.

Two weeks after Christmas my mother-in-law became ill and admitted to hospital. We did not realise it was anything serious but when I went to visit her she looked quite poorly. Jim went to visit her shortly afterwards and he and his family were told the bad news that she had incurable cancer and did not have long to live. It all happened so suddenly. She died within two weeks and it was a terrible shock to everyone. I felt devastated I had lost a good friend. The shock caused Jim severe eczema problems. He had difficulty sleeping and instead of prescribing him sleeping tablets, his doctor advised him to have a drink to enable him to sleep.

Unfortunately, this was the worst thing that he could have suggested. Jim started to go to the pub night after night leaving me at home to look after Jill and watch the TV. I reached a point where I could have thrown a brick through the TV it was so boring.

I decided to do something constructive and started to do something I had not done for several years. Drawing and painting was in my blood and I decided that it might be a good idea for me to start painting and selling my work. I had been successful in selling my work years earlier as I sat and painted beside the canal. I started to paint Christmas presents. Then with our neighbour's niece who had come to stay for a while, I enrolled for evening classes in artwork. I was now expecting our second child.

It was not long before I was producing some reasonable artwork and had requests from friends and neighbours to complete orders for my work. This income was very useful. My college course ended and I received much encouragement from my tutors, which gave me confidence in what I was doing.

CHAPTER 4

My career as an artist

I must have been about seven months pregnant and I was worried about Jill who had a high temperature and seemed lifeless. I was not sure what was wrong but the weather was cold outside and we did not have a car to take her to the doctors. I rang them to see if the doctor would come out and examine her. When the doctor arrived, she was furious that I had called her out and was very unpleasant towards me. I was in tears when she left, and was upset and reeling from shock that she was so hard and uncompassionate.

As I was at home, the decorating was left to me to do and Jim did not offer to lift a finger to help me with this. I was heavily pregnant by now but our new baby's room needed decorating. I set to and painted it from top to bottom and as the days got nearer for her to be born, I put some finishing touches to her room in way of nursery rhyme illustrations. This last effort was too much. I should have been resting with my feet up at this time and my ankles and feet swelled up forcing me to start resting.

Determined the birth of my second child would be easier than my first I had tried to look after my health and did plenty of breathing and relaxation exercises in readiness. I also ate a healthy diet and took supplements to enhance nutrition for my body to absorb.

I had to go for a check-up at my doctor's on the day Kate was due to be born. The surgery was about one and a half miles away. We had no transport and there were no buses that went along that route so I had to walk and push Jill in her pram to the surgery. After the examination, I started to feel contractions and asked the receptionist if I could use the phone, if I paid for the call, to ring my mother to come over and look after Jill. My mother lived 18 miles away and had to come by bus, train and bus to arrive at our home. The receptionist refused and I was in tears as I walked to the nearest phone box to call her. The phone was out of order so I had to go back to the surgery and ask the receptionist again. This time she relented, but she had quite a bad attitude for no apparent reason, because it was about two o clock in the afternoon and the surgery was quite empty. Thankfully, my mother was able to come over in time to look after Jill before I was taken to hospital.

I had a trouble free time when my second daughter arrived. We named her after her grandmother who she sadly would never be able to see. The day she was born Jim told me that he and all the plant where he worked were out on strike. This was due to unfair management tactics imposed on the employees, rushing their work through without it being finished properly, and then blaming the employees for shoddy work. I was a little concerned about this but also worried about the skin problems our second child seemed to have. She had such dry skin that when I bathed her I was told by the nurses not to use soap just water to cleanse her.

We returned home and as Jim was unable to work, he took charge of Kate's care while I completed some oil painting commissions and sold them. Then Jim managed to take on a window cleaning round while the window cleaner was in hospital and recovering from an operation. It was a struggle but we managed somehow throughout the twelve-week strike that Jim and his fellow workers were locked into. I was very thankful to God for looking after us.

It was about this time that I became aware of the way that Jim's younger brother Simon was becoming so very thin. I became very concerned about him, told Jim, and his father that perhaps he was not recovering very well from the shock and loss of his mother and perhaps needed some help in this. They seemed sceptical and took no notice of what I said.

Several months later, we learned the sad news that Simon was also was suffering from cancer and there seemed to be very little anyone could do. We were devastated, he was only fourteen years old. Jim's eczema became so severe it covered his whole body. He could not sleep at night but continued to work in a very demanding job. At the weekends, he was totally exhausted and he would lie on the sofa and sleep most of the time. I knew he could not carry on like this. His doctor had been of very little help with his eczema and his inability to be able to sleep, in fact, he had suggested that he drink alcohol to enable him to sleep. This was about the most unhelpful thing he could have said. We were struggling to pay bills but Jim was spending more money on going out for a drink just to help him sleep. I had to go to the mortgage lender and burst into tears before they would enable me to pay what we owed in more affordable instalments. I found it very difficult to communicate with my husband properly any more. He did not talk to me unless I spoke to him first. As I was praying for him one day, I remembered the acupuncture doctor I had received treatment from nearly ten years earlier. I prayed further as I could not afford to pay for private treatment. I felt the Lord was leading me to contact the acupuncture doctor and ask if I could hang my paintings in his clinic for sale and pay for Jim's treatment in this way. I anxiously rang the clinic and put this idea to the doctor there. He was a kind and compassionate man and to my amazement he agreed to this and booked Jim in for treatment the next week. A friend took him for this first treatment and the doctor told him that he was on the verge of a mental and physical breakdown and if he had left it another week it might have been too late. I thanked God for his foresight and a way out of this desperate situation.

The acupuncture treatment was very successful in that it restored his body to its natural balance and brought back his energy levels and allowed him to sleep better, but it did not completely clear Jim's eczema. He was told by the doctor, who was a fully qualified G.P. as well as an acupuncture doctor, that because he was not prepared to stop drinking alcohol that this irritant to his body was causing the eczema. Sadly, Jim would not listen to either the knowledgeable acupuncture doctor or myself and carried on drinking. Satisfied that I had done all I could at that time I knew I had to leave it to Jim to sort out himself but imagine my amazement when my paintings sold and Jim's treatment was paid for. I was so thankful and gave thanks to God once again for His compassion and love for us.

We now had two children to support and from time to time Jim found himself on a three or four day week because the company he was working for were having some problems, so I felt the need to be able to work regularly. One morning while I was praying I felt the Lord suggest to me that I have an exhibition of my work. Hopefully I would be able to sell some of it and perhaps receive some commissions so it was advertised in the local paper and set up in a local building society. I received an amazing response both selling several pieces of work at the exhibition and receiving commissions that would keep me in regular work for four years! Despite the sadness we were going through at that time I praised the Lord for the way in which he was providing for us.

I felt a need to spend more time with Jill and Kate and decided to take a little longer over my paintings. I was glad I was able to do this. I wanted to feel calmer and more relaxed and not under a lot of stress.

Our home needed some work doing to it. The kitchen needed the bare brick wall plastering. It was such an unsightly mess. Jim repeatedly ignored the request for him to do this. I bought some plaster and attempted to do this myself, but I did not make a very good job of it. Jim eventually finished the work off that I had started.

Kate was a complete contrast to her older sister. She used to wake several times a night. I found it difficult to use any routine for her feeding. When she was about five and a half weeks old, our doctor advised me to supplement her feeds with cow's milk. This gave her wind, but she seemed more satisfied. When it was time for me to start feeding her solids I did exactly the same as I had for Jill and blended down the same food that we ate which I always made myself from good quality food, full of nutrition and fed this to her. Within a week, she broke out in eczema on her back, legs and face. I was worried about her, felt quite helpless, and prayed for her to be free of these awful skin problems.

Our health visitor advised me to discard the cortisone cream our doctor had prescribed for her because of the harm it could do to her skin. She gave me a diet sheet to test her for allergies to food. This meant substituting cow's milk for goat's milk and trying a range of foods, a category at a time for 10–14 days. This was very successful and I soon learned the foods to avoid which assisted her in having a good night's sleep. Her skin improved considerably and I was very relieved and thanked the Lord once again for His blessings upon us.

Simon's health was deteriorating further and as he was by now spending long periods of time on his own at home I decided to go over with Jill and Kate and get him a meal at midday when his father and sister were out at work. We needed to catch two buses each way to my father-in-law's home. I spent some time praying for Simon and took holy water from Lourdes brought back by our neighbour especially for him. I wrote to Pope John Paul II hoping that his prayers for Simon would bring about the healing that we all hoped would happen. I even considered becoming a Catholic as Jim and his family had been brought up in this faith.

Jim was reluctant to go and see his younger brother in case he broke down in front of him. His married sister was disgusted that he did not see Simon very often and had no understanding of the suffering that Jim was experiencing. His younger sister by now was caring for him. It must have been very difficult for her to cope with, but she seemed to manage very well at the time.

Jill fell over her and grazed her knee. I tried to comfort her but she seemed quite distressed. I gingerly washed it and was about to dress it with antiseptic and a plaster when I kissed it better. She stopped crying and cheered up. I had just recovered from having a cold sore and it had just about healed up.

The next day Jill showed me a large itchy spot on her wrist I did not think a great deal about it. The next day it was worse and looked quite swollen. When I took her to see the doctor, he was concerned about Jill's wrist, particularly as she was running a high temperature. He said that she would have to be admitted to hospital for investigation into what was wrong. I was devastated.

There was only a junior doctor on duty when Jill was examined on the ward. He seemed puzzled and spoke about a lumbar puncture. I became anxious. Jill's temperature was 39.5°C and the nurses were clearly concerned. They undressed her and kept a fan on her all night. I stayed with her and half way through the night knelt down on my knees and prayed to Jesus to heal Jill.

The following morning her temperature had dropped dramatically and one of the nurses, who had noticed me praying, cheerfully said that God has answered your prayers. I was so thankful. That morning a skin specialist was in the hospital and was called to the ward to examine Jill. He immediately recognised what was wrong asking me if my husband or I had suffered with a cold sore. I told him what had happened when Jill grazed her knee and he very kindly told me not to blame myself. Thankfully, he was able to prescribe the medication that Jill needed and I stayed to help the nurses with her care. This involved bathing her skin where these spots had emerged all over her body. On the third day, the nurses insisted that I go home to rest as I had not really slept because I was so worried about her.

After I had received a good night's sleep I made a fuss of Kate who I had missed so much and to my horror found that she too was starting to suffer with the same problem as spots erupted on her skin. I took her to our doctor who immediately arranged for her and her sister to be transferred to an isolation ward and for provision for me to stay there with them.

We were so relieved when our daughters were discharged from hospital and fully recovered. The specialist told us that it was possible that this could happen again but it would never affect our daughters as severely again as their immune systems would be able to handle it better next time. He gave me some special treatment to use if I ever had a cold sore again.

Two weeks later after I felt that Kate was fully recovered from her ordeal I took her back to playgroup. While I was coming away, I heard a child there with a very bad cough. I felt uneasy leaving her wondering if because she had been so weak she might be more vulnerable to germs. I felt angry with the parents who had left this child amongst all the other children. I wondered if I was overreacting and left her there for the morning. It was a big mistake. The child with the bad cough was suffering from whooping cough and Kate now contracted that and was given more antibiotics and penicillin to get her through this with as little damage as possible to her chest and lungs. Of course, Jill caught it as well and once again, I had to nurse them both. I thanked God that they both came through this without too much difficulty.

About a week later, I noticed that Kate was suffering once again with eczema. Our health visitor suggested that I ask our skin specialist for a referral to the hospital dietitian, but the skin specialist was reluctant to do this and could not understand how the dietitian could help my daughter's eczema, but eventually he agreed.

About a week later, we met the dietitian who was very kind and understanding and made Kate feel at her ease. Mrs Masters was very thorough weighing Kate and measuring her height to ascertain her normal growth. She said it was necessary to put Kate on a low allergen diet for two weeks and slowly introduce one item of food in the correct order at a time each fortnight. As the diet was so restrictive calcium and other supplements were provided to make sure she received adequate nutrition. This enabled us to see quite clearly the food and drinks that Kate was allergic to. She had now become allergic to many more food items. I did the best I could to make her food look the same as ours because I did not want her to feel different. Once we had established what her allergies were, her eczema receded and she was a lot more comfortable. This was a great blessing to see that this worked and to see Kate smiling and happy again. It took a lot of effort to implement this restricted diet but now it had proved worth it.

Although for years after Jim and I were first married, we never had any arguments. These were now becoming more and more frequent and devastating. I found that it took me several days to get over the upset and during that time, I could not function to work on my oil paintings.

When we saw Simon again he looked very frail and thin and it tore at our hearts seeing him like that. It made us feel so helpless. We always tried to make him feel positive about his recovery but inwardly we felt dismayed as he continued to deteriorate. His specialists at the hospital seemed callous, in telling such a young person what was wrong with him, making no allowance for the fact that his mother had died from the same type of cancer only two years previously. I rang one of them and asked her if she knew what had happened to Simon's mother and apparently, she had no knowledge of this. When I told her, she realised how cruel it had been to tell him what was wrong with him and give him no hope. A week later, she visited him at home and told him that he was going to recover and his health was improving.

Shortly afterwards he died. We were all heartbroken. I felt angry with God and could not understand why he had allowed this to happen. Jim's sisters fell out with us, they did not notify us when he died and we found out from a neighbour who saw it in the newspaper. Jim's family seemed quite oblivious to the difficulties we were experiencing as a family.

My husband and I remained in this dark cloud for about eight months. We stopped going to church. I was very angry with God and one day I shouted at Him, demanding answers as to why people get cancer and if there was any way that it could be prevented.

I am sure that He heard me because a few days later information that I had no knowledge of kept flooding my head about pollution and how man is damaging his own health. I seemed to be hearing that there was pollution in our food and water and the air we breathed due to man's exploitation of the earth, which in turn was leading to cancer and many other serious illnesses.

One day there was a knock on our door, I answered it. A young man was standing there speaking in an American accent he introduced himself as Max and told me that he had come over for a year to assist our local Methodist minister, and was calling to see how we were. I invited him in introduced him to Jill and Kate and went on to explain how I felt that God had abandoned us and allowed Simon to die. He encouraged us to go to church again, told me about a prayer group that he was starting up and invited me to that.

After he had left, I still felt angry and kept thinking about all the suffering that Simon had gone through. That was all I could think about. I threw myself into my work and tried not to think. Jim and I laughed very little anymore. The only thing that cheered us up was our two daughters, who were so lively and full of fun.

About a month later Max called on us again. He tried to encourage me to come along to the prayer group that was now running but I told him that I was not interested as inwardly I still felt a real bitterness in my heart. I had got on so well with my mother-in-law who was such a lovely person, so kind and a real friend. She taught me how to make some delicious meals and always had time to talk to me. It had always been such a pleasure to see her and the rest of Jim's family before she died. I was heartbroken when she died so suddenly and so young at only 52 years of age. When Simon fell ill with the same deadly illness it just felt as though the bottom had dropped out of our lives. Simon also had a lovely nature, like his Mum, and I got on well with him as well. He used to like going fishing with Jim. Why, I asked God was this happening to Jim's family?

Another month went by and once more Max knocked on our door. He did not give up easily and once more, he invited me to the prayer group that he had set up and told me that if only I would come along once that he was sure that I would receive great comfort and peace. I reluctantly agreed to go along.

As I entered the house where the prayer meeting was to take place, everyone there warmly welcomed me. There was a real warmth and friendship amongst these people, which amazed me. Max led the meeting and I felt myself crying through most of it, as I struggled to explain to concerned friends there, how Simon's death had affected my husband and myself. Prayers were said for us as a family and for many people in need of prayer. Afterwards was a time of sharing. I was glad that I made the effort, went to that meeting, and was filled with peace as I left. As I was leaving I was invited to an ecumenical renewal service at the local Anglican church which was to take place the following week.

The evening of the renewal service arrived and Betty and Joan called for me and took me along. As I entered the church with them, I noticed that it was full to capacity with

Christians from many different denominations. There was such a peaceful atmosphere.

The service began with praising songs and those singing in tongues sounded like angels singing. Time seemed to stand still and at the end of the service the speaker encouraged people to come forward for healing but I was quite determined that nothing would make me go forward and stayed where I was.

More and more people went up for prayer but I stubbornly remained standing near the back of the church. Suddenly it felt as though God had picked me up and brought me to the front of the church. I don't remember explaining to the healing ministers why I wanted prayer, I thought, God knows why. It was a very emotional time, but as they prayed for me, I was filled with a real inner peace and a sense of God's presence.

I returned home and explained to Jim what had happened, but he seemed sceptical and seemed to miss the whole point. He appeared still to feel inwardly very bitter.

Four days later, something very special happened. I was lying awake in bed thinking about getting up. Suddenly an amazing peace descended on me something that felt as though it was not of this world then I saw a picture of Simon in Heaven surrounded by a white light. He was smiling and looked the picture of health and happiness. I thought I heard a voice which said to me 'Now will you stop worrying about Simon, he is fine.' The vision disappeared but the peace remained with me for a while. I couldn't believe what had happened. My icy attitude towards God started to melt and I thanked Him for this wonderful experience and His reassurance.

I started to put the sadness that I felt about Simon behind me. I felt that I needed to trust in the Lord, but I still needed to know why this had happened and questioned God over and over until I felt him speaking to me and giving me answers. I felt that he was telling me that a combination of pollution in our water, food and the atmosphere was contributing to so many people suffering from cancer, and it was as though He was trying to tell me to take great care of my own family and to look after their health. I told Jim about the picture but he seemed to be indifferent and locked into the same woundedness that I had been ensnared in before I had received the healing and insight that my Heavenly Father had given to me.

CHAPTER 5

My prayer life became more important to me

I felt led by the Holy Spirit to visit Joan and Kevin my sister and brother-in-law to try to explain to them the difficulties we had gone through and how Jim had been so badly affected by his brother's illness and death. I asked the Lord to go with me. I knew that they had very little, if any Christian faith and did not see things in the same way that I did. I asked the Lord to speak through me to them and I was very nervous about approaching them. When I arrived, they were pleasant towards me but not over-friendly. As I left I felt a peace and knew that the Lord had helped me in this difficult situation. I continued to pray for a family reconciliation.

About this time, we were encouraged to receive a full immersion adult baptism at the church that we attended. I prayed about this and felt that this was something that the Lord really wanted me to do. I went along to classes and found that several other like-minded people were going to join me in this. The baptism took place at the Elim church where my friend Rose and her family worshipped. This baptism really meant something to me. During the classes, I renounced my involvement when I was younger in activities that I was now ashamed of namely going to a fortune teller, allowing a friend at work to read my cards and taking part in something similar to a Ouija board game. I went along to the baptism praying that I had been washed clean of all my sins and could start afresh. It was a very good feeling, a peaceful and happy time.

I asked Jim if he would like to go to a fellowship meeting, but he refused. Thankfully, he and our children were prayed for regularly at these meetings. I searched the Christian bookshop hoping that I could find something that might help and found a book which described what happens when people suffer wounds in their life and likened it to a tree that has been severely damaged, and needs nurturing and love to aid healing. I did my best to help Jim in all sorts of ways, but it felt as though he did not want anyone's help. It seemed as though he just wanted to be left alone to suffer. He refused to talk about, or have any photos of, his mother or brother in the house.

Max came to our house one day for a meal. After he had left, Jim was amazed at his enthusiasm and agreed to go to the next ecumenical renewal service at the Anglican church. Unfortunately, when it came to the day Jim was reluctant to go. He did not enjoy the service or have any wish to go forward for prayer.

It was now the end of Max's stay in England and he was returning to the States. Many of us would miss his encouragement.

We regularly saw my parents. Usually they came over to see us as we did not have our own car at this time and it was quite a lengthy journey on public transport. I now seemed to be able to get on well with my father who used to be so distant and reluctant to communicate with me. However, I now know that this was his way of extracting information about us and our family life so that he could sabotage our lives.

I enjoyed my mother's company and always looked forward to seeing her. We had a lot in common in our Christian faith, and used to share our experiences.

Jill had now started school and had met some lovely friends there. It was a church school and seemed very caring with high standards. I was able to have a chat with some of the other mothers when taking Jill to and from school. Four of us became really good friends and although we all worshipped in different churches that did not matter because we all had a common Christian faith. I found Rose very encouraging. Sometimes she invited me for a coffee and we shared our Christian faith. She and her family attended the Pentecostal church. We often prayed together which was very helpful because sometimes I was in need of prayer, as I was finding it difficult coping with Jim, still unable to come to terms with what had happened to his family.

Within our fellowship group, we prayed for the sick. There was a young man who had come to stay with one of the elderly members of our group. He was suffering with MS, was in a wheelchair and found it difficult to speak and to move about. We all decided to lay hands on him as a group and prayed for him. Nothing immediate happened, but before our next meeting, he was also taken to a healing meeting at a church in a nearby town. He was instantly healed and was able to walk and speak normally. When he came along to our next meeting, we were all overjoyed.

The fellowship meeting continued, but we discovered that we had a wolf in sheep's clothing, in the form of the only man that now attended. We were shocked to find out that he had sexually assaulted the thirteen-year-old daughter of one of our members. We were concerned because our two daughters attended the Sunday School and he went to church each Sunday. Our minister refused to do anything about this so we felt we had no choice but to leave the Methodist church. I felt a great sadness about this as I had been brought up within the Methodist church and I missed it very much. We were without a church for a while and I prayed for guidance.

I returned home from town on the bus loaded down with shopping. Suddenly it felt as though the Lord was speaking to me and He seemed to be saying that our city was about to go through a severe decline. Jobs would be lost, the whole area would suffer, and people would become very depressed. In the media there also seemed to be a growing threat of a nuclear war. This bleak picture remained with me for a while and then I thought about the possibility of emigrating to Australia or New Zealand.

Later I tried to tell my husband what had happened but he did not understand and was sceptical. He did agree though to the possibility of emigrating and to possibly finding a better life abroad. After applying to emigrate to Australia, we were refused because we were classed as semi-skilled and not skilled or professional. I felt that Jim might be happier in another job, and that he might find more stability, but he remained where he was.

Jill was by now eight years old and I decided to start teaching her the piano. One of my dad's relatives gave us their piano. I had not played for about twenty years but decided to start playing again. Jill seemed to enjoy learning and took to it really well.

I felt drawn to go to the Anglican church where I had experienced my healing. I took Jill and Kate to the Sunday school there and attended the service. I felt at home as though the Lord was welcoming us into this church. It did not feel strange at all as other members of the congregation and the Sunday school teachers welcomed us so warmly. At communion, the children came back into church and went forward with their parents for a blessing. Occasionally a member of the congregation would stand and give a message in tongues to the whole church, which was translated into English for everyone to understand. This was amazing, and the messages were full of hope and encouragement from the Lord. I thought to myself if only I could encourage Jim to come back to church again I was sure it would help him. I returned home in tears a couple of Sundays and he wanted to know what was wrong so I told him that I really missed him not going to church with me and he promised to go with me again soon. I continued going each week with Jill and Kate and occasionally Jim came as well, but he never seemed to feel comfortable in this church.

One day at the school gates Angela, one of our Christian friends, came along looking very worried and told us about a family who were in real need of prayer. The daughter of her friend was about twenty-one years old and was in hospital in a coma and on a life support machine. Her family were devastated and did not know what was wrong. We agreed to pray for this young woman at about 6 pm that evening when Angela was going to the hospital to lay hands on her and pray for her there. We found out afterwards that whole churches were praying for her across the city.

Amazingly, the following day she opened her eyes and later that day was able to hold hands and then started to speak. As she continued to recover, a jubilant nurse said to Angela that this was the first time that she had taken anyone off a life support machine who had recovered. We were all very thankful to the Lord for this miracle and learned afterwards that the poor woman had been suffering from three life threatening illnesses at once scarlet fever, rheumatic fever and glandular fever.

My friend Rose who was a member of the Pentecostal church invited us along to her church to see if Jim felt more comfortable there. We all went along and Jill and Kate happily settled in the Sunday school. Rose whose daughter was in the same class at school as Jill, made us feel welcome here. Jim seemed more settled in this church although it was very different to any he had been to before. Soon we met other members of the congregation and one couple in particular were very encouraging. They came to our home and invited us to theirs for meals. They did all they could to encourage us and one day Jane informed us that the Lord had told her that Jim and I were to become evangelists. They invited us to a special meeting to listen to a team of evangelists from America whose interesting talk captivated us. One spoke while the other painted a beautiful scene of the area that they had come from, which showed a beautiful lake and mountain range. As one of them spoke, we learned that tragically he had lost two members of his family. Jim sat up and listened to this valuable witness and the positive way that this man spoke of how the Lord had given him great strength, comfort and peace and of how the Lord loves him and it was not His will that these tragedies happened.

Jim seemed transformed by the witness that was given and when we arrived home, he said that he wanted to commit his life to Jesus and do it properly. On a daily basis, he set about reading the Bible from cover to cover but something sinister started to happen. One evening when he was reading he started to shake violently, he become very agitated, his eczema flared up and he started to scratch his skin like never before. I was shocked and could not understand what was happening at that time.

On another occasion, I listened with interest to a sermon at our new church about how Satan can attack people and how we should be able to pray confidently for Jesus's protection. He also mentioned witchcraft and how there was a need to pray against this because there seemed to be a lot of occult interest these days. He told us how he had come across a group of Satan worshippers, which was quite disturbing, and when I returned home I did pray about this situation but a frightening thing happened. The lights in our living room kept flickering and when I stopped praying about this the flickering stopped. I became afraid to pray against witchcraft anymore.

At the next opportunity I told Rose what had happened and she said that she would pray for the situation. She encouraged me to have a deeper faith and told me how she started each day in prayer. Sometimes she got up quite early to do this, even during the night occasionally spending time in front of the Lord, and felt blessed as a result. She encouraged me to take my faith more seriously.

After this, I started getting up at about 6 am each morning to pray. I noticed an instant difference. It felt as though if I spent time in front of the Lord at the beginning of the day it went more smoothly and I seemed to have more time to do things. I felt a real peace and continued in this way.

I was still concerned about the flickering lights so when I heard about a healing course at the parish church in the city run by a well-known minister and his team I enrolled. I found the course eye-opening and very interesting. As a small group, we sat in a circle waiting on the Lord for a word or a picture for any members of the small congregation who were coming along to our evening healing service. Several of us had a 'word' or a 'picture', which were read out during the service. This helped people who had come for healing to have more confidence, to enable them to come forward during the service, and discuss with us what the Holy Spirit had revealed to us.

Our children were growing up and were doing well at school so for a special treat we decided to let them have a pet. They were excited, as they loved animals so we contacted a well-known cat rescue organisation. We were offered a black long-haired kitten who was beautiful. Our children were fascinated by him and helped to care for him. He was very entertaining and full of fun.

We decided that it would be a good idea for our children to learn to swim and took them to the swimming pool. Jim encouraged them to submerge themselves in the water and played with them so that they were not afraid. We helped them to learn the swimming strokes and encouraged them until eventually, several weeks later they both managed to start swimming. We continued to take them regularly to practise their swimming.

Meanwhile, Jim became less willing to go to church and stopped going altogether. I could not understand what was going on. I knew I could not force him to go to church but I was very upset he had now turned his back on Christ.

Something else strange happened. My friend Rose and I were both experiencing similar difficulties at work. She and I both felt abnormal and completely out of character attractions to male colleagues there. We did not want to feel like this but the feelings were powerful. She had confided in me when I had told her of my experiences. I did not know what to do but I felt that I needed help. I decided to tell Jim what was happening and ask him to pray for me. We prayed together and he prayed for me regularly. The news of this, however, was too much for Jim to bear and he became very low and clingy. He started to mistrust me and used this against me for many years to come. I told Rose that I had felt led by the Lord to tell Jim and ask him for prayer support and that she perhaps should do the same. She fell out with me soon afterwards after she had told her husband although he was very understanding and told her that she had done the right thing.

Something spooky that unsettled me for some years was an unexplained shadow over Jim's side of our bed in the shape of a coffin. I could not understand this and used to pray for Jim's protection. Also, a doll given to Jill as a present from my parents was giving her some distress. She said that it moved its eyes and she was scared of it. Her fear seemed quite genuine and she told me to take it out of her room. I tried to reassure her and was quite sure that her imagination was playing tricks on her. I used to get up early to cook Jim's breakfast and get him off to work and then spend time in prayer. This seemed to help me feel settled for the day.

An opportunity arose for us to move back to my home town, but the property, which we had been offered, was too expensive and we could not afford it. My father offered to lend us some money towards it and pay a small percentage of the mortgage for a while. The interest rate at that time was very high. Jim was reluctant about this. I prayed for guidance and felt that the Lord wanted us to move to this semi-detached house on the edge of the countryside with a large garden and an allotment.

Jim eventually agreed and we moved house during May. It was a lovely sunny day and here we were at last in the countryside that we had missed so much. We hoped that our daughters would enjoy their country upbringing.

Within a few days of moving Kate became ill with a bad chest infection. She had to stay in bed for a fortnight before it started to clear. It was an unexpected worry. Worse still, this continued to happen on a regular basis throughout the summer.

The new secretarial job that I had been promised unfortunately fell through so I was now left without work. I decided to go back to my artwork and after advertising obtained some commissions. As I enjoyed painting so much I was glad to be able to work from home and be there for our daughters when they came home from school.

Our daughters soon started at the local school that had a good reputation. They seemed to settle in nicely and make friends with the local children.

CHAPTER 6

Producing dairy-free chocolate

By the time September came, we were very concerned about Kate's health. After being admitted to hospital, her health did not improve. I noticed a poster in the hospital about a talk being given by an allergy specialist the following week at a hospital close by. I made a decision to go along.

I apprehensively arrived for the talk and hoped that I would be able to extract some useful information from it. The hall was crammed and the talk very informative. I took notes, and realised once again that diet was so important in eliminating allergies. The specialist explained how asthma, eczema and even dyslexia could be caused through allergies to certain foods. We had hoped that Kate was fully recovered from all her food allergies. I went home and started to organise a change to Kate's diet, reverting to the low allergen diet that had improved her health when she was much younger.

She returned from hospital a few days later with the same bad chest infection and asthma that had caused her admittance to hospital. I told her what I planned to do to help her and she was quite happy about this. Almost three days later, the chest infection had disappeared, Kate was laughing and playing as though nothing had been wrong. The transformation was unbelievable. It was a shame that the specialists at our hospital did not seem to recognise the benefits of removing allergens from a child's diet. I was glad that I had the support of the dietician when we lived at the nearby city where Kate and Jill were born.

It was mid-morning and a knock came at the door. I opened it and there stood an irate woman who went on to say that my eldest daughter Jill had been upsetting her daughter. She went on in quite a threatening and intimidating way and left. I was shocked. What she had described was not my daughter, I did not believe that she had it in her to be so unpleasant to others.

That afternoon I questioned Jill. She told me that this particular girl was ill treated at home and was made to go out and play with her brother in all weathers and rarely allowed into their home. This girl was a loner and she was the one who had been unpleasant to Jill, who had just tried to stick up for herself. I told her not to worry and to avoid all contact with this problem child, but I did feel sorry for the girl who was badly treated by her mother.

Over the next two or three years I managed to sell quite a few of my oil paintings. I had a stall at a nearby national show and from the interest I received, I started to do talks as well which gave me more work.

I also looked into another project that I had started when the children were quite small.

When Kate had been quite little, she had a milk and dairy allergy and could not tolerate Easter eggs or Christmas chocolate tree novelties. I felt sorry for her because I could remember how as a child I had enjoyed these luxuries. A friend suggested that perhaps I could go to the market in the town where we lived then, where there was a homemade sweet stall and ask the stallholder if he could possibly make Kate some milk-free chocolate. This seemed like a good idea so I went to the market and asked him if he could help. He said that he would love to help, but it would not be worth his while making such a small amount of chocolate. He kindly gave me some hardened palm kernel oil and told me the ingredients he used in his chocolate, but he said that he could not give me his recipe, as this would not be fair.

I returned home and prayed for guidance as to the correct quantities to use. Unbelievably on the first attempt, I was amazed and thankful to find that the chocolate that I had made tasted really good. I thanked the Lord for His guidance. I then went on to try making a slightly different chocolate with a little more of Kate's soya milk. This also came out very well and was lighter and more like the chocolate bought in the shops.

Sometime later, I also experimented with chocolate made with carob instead of cocoa. This was a success as well. When our friends found out, some of them told me about other children who also had dairy allergies and I made chocolate not just for Kate but for quite a few other children as well.

Now in our new home I felt the Lord was leading me to think about the possibility of chocolate being produced on a larger scale as there were so many children that I had come across with dairy allergies. After praying about this I bought some moulds, made bars of chocolate wrapped and labelled them and left them to stand to test their shelf life.

I also went into town with a survey that I had written out and surveyed about twenty people to see what their reaction was to our chocolate. Everyone seemed to like it and I had some good feedback with it compared to many of the High Street brands in the shops. After analysing the results of the survey I produced some paperwork to show how viable it might be to produce dairy free chocolate as at that time 4% of the population were dairy intolerant.

By this time, Jim had put a new kitchen into our home and it had been designed with the possibility of producing chocolate as a cottage industry in mind.

While I was trying to find out prices of the products I needed, to produce the chocolate, I was in contact with a Belgian company, which supplied the palm kernel oil. This company were interested in our chocolate and invited me to go down to their experimental plant in London to have our chocolate made professionally. The soya milk manufacturer's director was very interested too because his son was allergic to diary produce. He was very supportive and gave me a good price for this product in bulk.

A few weeks later, I went down to London to see the trials of our chocolate made professionally. It was exciting. The staff at the lab were quite enthusiastic about it all and taught me how to temper chocolate. They also showed me the different types of palm kernel oil they had and gave me advice on the best type to produce our chocolate.

When I returned home, I contacted three of the main chocolate manufacturers. I found a solicitor who gave me advice on patenting the recipes and drew up a legal document for a prospective chocolate manufacturer to sign for our recipes, so that I could receive royalties as it was being produced and retailed.

I contacted the chairman of one of these companies and was invited to meet with two of the directors there. I attended the meeting with my paperwork, a properly worded legal document in case they were interested in buying the recipes and of course samples of our chocolate for them to try.

They seemed impressed, but said that their operations were on such a large scale that 4% of the population – which is what I had based my figures on – was too small a project for them to consider. They did, however, try to persuade me to let them see the recipe and have a copy of it. I refused and was upset by their underhanded tactics. I returned home feeling rather disappointed and disgusted.

About two weeks later the second chocolate manufacturer invited me to their production factory. These people were pleasant and interested, but told me that they too were under an enormous amount of pressure from their competitors. If they adopted this specialised small-scale project and it failed, this would not look good for their image.

Finally, the third manufacturer was interested in our chocolate but said that they would only take it on if it was made with cocoa butter. Sadly, ours had been refined with special hardened palm kernel oil.

I did not want to give up and found a chocolate manufacturing seminar at a well-known food college. The course that I attended which lasted two days was quite expensive, but I managed to raise the money for this. It was very interesting but as I did not have the necessary technical knowledge, I found it quite hard to relate to. Taking notes, I hoped that it would all fit into place later as I became more knowledgeable about chocolate, and hopefully have more practical experience. After the course, I spoke to a couple of the organisers about my chocolate and they were quite interested. One of them told me of a small machine that they had invented and produced themselves suitable for use in small-scale chocolate manufacture. They said that they would be in touch about this.

A few weeks later, I was invited back to the college to put our chocolate through the machinery there as well. The chocolate came out very smooth and seemed just as good as when made at the other lab. There was just one drawback, in that this machine used ball bearings in the refining of the chocolate and I wondered if this could be a potential health hazard for any of our customers if a stray ball bearing ever found its way into the chocolate bars that we produced.

My parents were interested in what was going on and surprisingly my father offered to lend me the full amount that I needed to buy this machine, as it was out of my price range.

When it came to me placing the order for the chocolate making machine my father, inexplicably lost his temper and denied he had ever offered to help fund the cost of the machine to produce the chocolate. Sadly, our plans to produce dairy-free chocolate were scrapped, as there was no way that I could afford to pay for this equipment myself. Our income from my oil paintings along with Jim's wages were going into our family budget to feed and clothe us all and of course pay our bills and there was very little left over.

Sometimes after Jim had been drinking, he became abusive towards me. I could not understand why. It felt as though he was taking out on me all the aggression he felt inside at his sisters' rejection and unfair accusations of him. Even his father did not seem the same towards him anymore. I used to send them lovely birthday and Christmas presents, hoping and continuing to pray for a healing in our relationships. We continued to visit his dad regularly and he came to visit us for dinner and tea sometimes at the weekend.

I decided that I would like to return to the Methodist church that I had grown up in. I took Jill and Kate to Sunday school there each week, and joined my mother once again in the congregation. At about this time I felt the Lord was leading me to start studying as a local preacher. I thoroughly enjoyed this and seemed to be getting on quite well with it. I went to several churches to lead services as I trained under the watchful eye of a friend and local preacher who had known Jim and I for years.

During the winter months, Kate was fine. The low allergen diet had done its job and now she was able to eat normally again. Jim had planted out the garden and allotment during the summer and we had an abundance of homegrown fresh or frozen fruit and vegetables which lasted all year through.

Jill was doing very well now on the piano and I asked Kate if she would like to learn as well but she was not sure, so I said why don't you try and see if you enjoy it. She did enjoy learning but seemed to have less patience than her elder sister. It was lovely to hear them both playing music.

I was invited to a meeting of the clergy and local preachers in our main church in town. I can remember being shocked at their apparent lack of willingness to move on and be open to the Holy Spirit leading us forward. After praying about this, I made several suggestions, the main one being ecumenical healing services in all the town churches in turn. After the open mindedness I had experienced in the nearby city's churches we had left, this did not seem too radical, but our church in this town seemed to be full of narrow-minded clergy who were not open to the Holy Spirit's guidance.

About a year into my training, and after several more similar meetings, I felt the only way forward for me was to resign, as my suggestions were rejected with no compromise. Another trainee local preacher tried to encourage me to continue, but I really felt the Lord was telling me that all I was doing was making myself unpopular, so I reluctantly left. This was a very painful time for me, as I loved what I was doing very much. Jim, though, never approved and now rarely came with me to church. My tutor who was based in the south of the country was upset and said that she would continue to pray for me and the situation in our town's churches.

Jim's drinking was still a problem and his abusive behaviour was affecting me quite badly. Several times, I slept downstairs because of this. On one occasion, I suffered a frightening experience when it felt as though I had been hurled off the sofa on to the floor. I woke up it had been a nightmare, but it did seem very real. I decided to contact Rev. Long who I had previously met at a healing ministry course at his Parish church in the city where we used to live. He specialised in deliverance healing and I wondered if this might help Jim. He kindly invited us both to his house. Jim was sceptical but he was fed up with all the rows and arguments we seemed to be having, and seemed unaware that this was fuelled by his abuse of alcohol.

Rev. Long's vicarage home was very basic. There seemed to be no room for materialism in his life. He made us feel at home and insisted on us calling him by his first name, Ian. He prayed for us both and then specifically for Jim, asking him about his father and grandparents. When he found out that Jim had a mining background he said that often stubbornness was a problem with those from mining stock and that deep-seated problems were sometimes difficult to deal with in these circumstances. He explained how our spirit can be damaged during our life through difficult situations we may encounter or through occult or pornography involvement resulting in the possibility of evil spirits taking the opportunity to alight on us if we are wounded. He also mentioned that if someone is under the influence of alcohol, this can be a way the enemy has a foothold in our life and demons and evil spirits can take over in these situations. He prayed for some time for Jim and in the Name of Jesus cast out alcohol and through the Holy Spirit's guidance asked him if he wanted to confess any pornography involvement, so that he could pray into this also. Jim denied this at the time and said that there was no such problem. I remembered the pornographic magazines and some of the stories he had told me about his past. I was sad that he refused prayer for this.

After the prayers were completed, we left thanking Ian and leaving him a donation. After this, Jim seemed a changed man. He drank less and when he did drink, it had no bad effect on him. I praised the Lord.

I was becoming increasingly concerned about our children's schooling. I regularly looked at their books and supported them if they had any difficulty with their homework, and I was alarmed when I discovered that their work was in fact no further forward than it had been two years ago in the previous school that they had attended. We made a decision to move them to a local Catholic school and hoped that this ethos would be more caring like the Christian school that they had left behind at our previous home.

After what happened in the Methodist church, I had started to think about changing to the Catholic church as well. I discussed this with Jim and our children and they all seemed to be happy about this. Jim of course had been brought up as a Catholic.

I took our two daughters to see the priest and explained that we would like to join the Catholic church. He seemed very pleasant, smiled, and said that of course we could. Welcoming us, he made us feel at home. He made an appointment for us to visit the junior school and meet the headmaster telling us that the girls would receive all the education they needed about the Catholic faith at school and I was invited to go along to the presbytery for classes to learn about the Catholic way of doing things. The headmaster was very pleasant and helpful showing us round the school. He seemed to understand about the problems that open-plan modern methods of teaching brought, where distractions got in the way of education.

Happily, Jill and Kate seemed to settle down quite well in their new school and made lots of friends.

One day the girls came home from school and asked if they could bring home a duckling or a chick each as they had hatched out in an incubator at school and all needed homes. As we did not have a pond, we agreed on two chicks who were very sweet. We soon realised that we needed a hen house and managed to buy a second-hand one. Jim made them a run and put chicken wire over the top as well so that there would be no danger of any foxes harming them. Eventually we were collecting two eggs a day from our chickens who our girls had named Sage and Onion.

Soon after we had joined the Catholic church, the priest happened to mention to me about the nuns at their convent in a small town nearby. Apparently, they produced their own chocolate to support themselves, and were having some difficulty with this at that time. When I told him of my interest in producing the dairy-free chocolate, he suggested that I get in contact with them.

Later that day I rang the convent and a friendly sounding sister answered the phone, her name was Sister Monica. She invited me to the convent to tell me about the halt to the production of their chocolate.

Two days later, I was shown round the convent, which was surrounded by beautiful countryside. The chapel was amazing and contained many items handmade by the sisters. Sister Monica took me to the outbuilding, which had been converted into a special kitchen, where the chocolate making was done. As we chatted about the convent and their failure to be able to continue to support themselves, it became obvious that there was something wrong here. First of all their chicken and egg producing business spectacularly crashed, when the retailers they were supplying to suddenly let them down. Undaunted they then decided to start making chocolates to sell locally.

Unfortunately this too was halted due to the sudden rise in the price of basic materials that they needed, making it impossible for them to continue to produce enough income to support their community. Then Sister Monica told me something very interesting about the former owners of the large country house that had now become their convent. It had been owned by the Lord of the Manor, whose wife was unfaithful to him and used to regularly travel down to the city. He eventually lost his temper with her and murdered her. She explained that a driver of one of the local lorry companies was one day driving down the road that passed the convent when he saw a woman on a horse galloping along the grass verge, but she overtook the lorry, which was travelling at sixty miles per hour. Apparently, he was so shocked and frightened that he drove the lorry straight to the depot and walked out of his job there and then.

A year or so later a monk of the same order as the sisters came over from America and learned about what had happened. He said some prayers over the woman's grave and she was never seen again. I told Sister Monica that I knew a minister in the Anglican church who was involved in deliverance healing and asked her if she thought it was a good idea to invite him to come and pray at the convent, as perhaps the man who committed the murder needed prayer. She said that she would have to ask Mother Superior, Sister Ruth's permission for this and I left saying that I would pray about the situation and she said that she would do the same.

A couple of days later I rang the convent and Sister Monica told me that Sister Ruth was happy for Rev. Long to come over and pray at the convent. Anxious to help the nuns I rang him as soon as I arrived home and asked if he could help. He said that he would be glad to and made arrangements to come over with a member of his healing ministry team to pray for the disturbed soul of this man who had murdered his wife.

Rev. Long and Helen, a member of his healing ministry team, arrived and were introduced to Sister Ruth. Rev. Long prayed at the site of the convent's previous owner's grave, the outbuildings and through the convent. He told us that the Holy

Spirit was telling him of the guilty conscience of this man and the pain he had suffered and how the prayers being said would now release him to go to Heaven. This man was responsible for all the problems that the nuns had experienced because he was a wandering lost soul. There was a sense of peace.

Several months later, I contacted Sister Monica again and asked how things were. She said that they had now found a new supplier for their raw materials enabling them to be able to start production again selling their chocolates and they had started doing bookbinding as well. They remained friendly and invited me to go and see them again. I stayed in touch with them for several years until we moved house and I was working full time.

CHAPTER 7

Pesticide poisoning affecting the neighbourhood

As spring approached, we noticed a decline in Kate's health again as she started to wheeze with asthma and her chest tightened up once again. There was farm spraying machinery travelling along our road, but did not think anything of it. We were concerned and puzzled as to why Kate was suffering so much. We thought it might be hay fever, but she had never suffered from that before. Just a few hundred yards away was a field of yellow rapeseed. Our next-door neighbour who had three young children told us of how she could not go out into the garden at this time of year or even throughout the summer months for fear of suffering in a similar way to Kate with severe hay fever symptoms.

I started to get migraine headaches quite often and joint pains. I started to find out that the turpentine that I was using to produce my oil paintings was making me worse but I persevered hoping that things would get better.

Jim's sister, Valerie got in touch with us and said that she wanted to come and see us. She was living with her boyfriend in Guernsey, but was returning to visit her Dad. She said that she regretted falling out with us and wanted us to be friends again. I was relieved and happy, and thanked the Lord for His answer to prayer. We all went out for a lovely meal together and caught up on each other's news.

That summer we went on holiday to a beautiful area of mountains and lakes. While we were there, we visited a rare breed farm and found some cute sheepdog puppies.

Some were herding ducks into the farm pond, they looked so funny and our daughters were captivated. They told us how much they would love to have one of these puppies. Jim and I smiled at each other, made a mental note and continued to enjoy our holiday. Kate seemed so much healthier in this environment especially when we reached the coast. It was lovely to see her look so happy. She played with her sister contentedly on the beach building sandcastles and paddling in the sea.

Jill had reached Grade II standard on the piano with my help, but now I was anxious for her to pass her exams. I took her to a qualified piano teacher, as I had only reached Grade V piano and theory and did not feel confident enough to put her through the piano exams myself. She was quickly prepared for her Grade I exam and passed it with ease because she was so competent. She continued with her lessons and soon Kate followed in her sister's footsteps and started to work for her Grade I exam.

Jill's teacher decided that she was doing so well that they would miss out Grade II and go on to Grade III. Both girls took their exams at the same time and passed, Kate achieved distinction and Jill did very well too.

Our neighbours June and Fred sometimes came round with their children on a Saturday evening and had a couple of drinks and some snacks with us while our children played. One evening Fred refused a drink of beer when Jim offered it to him because he said it now had a bad effect on him and had made him violent once or twice and he dare not drink it again. We wondered if it might be the chemicals that may have been put into the beer to give it a long shelf life.

My husband always seemed to have it in for Kate our youngest daughter. She struggled to eat her food sometimes because of her allergies returning, probably due to environmental problems where we lived. He was very unpleasant and repeatedly called her stupid. I was concerned about the long-term affect that this abuse would have on my child so I decided to get in touch with Rev. Long to ask if he could pray for her. He put me in touch with Helen who was a member of his prayer team who kindly offered to come to our home and pray for Kate. When she had finished praying for Kate and both children had gone out to play, I confided in her about some strange things that happened in our home. One day I noticed a strange noise that seemed to go from our living room, into our next-door neighbour's home and soon afterwards, they started to have a terrible row. It sent shivers down my spine at the time. I also had a strange experience one day when I felt as though I was being thrown off the settee while resting. She said that maybe the house needed praying for and arranged to come back and pray about this.

When Helen returned to pray for our house I told her that I felt perhaps, I needed some prayer too. Helen told me she could see a large claw above my head, which she felt through the Holy Spirit's guidance that this signified that my father had some sort of evil hold on me. She prayed for me in several sessions and I hoped that everything was now fine.

She suspected that something in the area, may also have a sinister connection, mentioning an institution in our town and possible Freemasonry activity in the area.

Four months later on Christmas morning, we woke up to our alarm clock at 5 am. Our children were already awake opening the Christmas pillowcases that Father Christmas had brought them! I got up, made breakfast for us all, and packed up a very special Christmas lunch to have on our journey.

We set off and told our daughters that we were going to see some friends. Eighty miles down the road Jill said, "That's funny I thought I saw a signpost directing us to the mountains and lakes. Where are these friends we are going to visit?"

I said, "Oh did you, well it is not much further to go now."

As we approached the farm, we were all able to recognise where we were going and the girls were very excited. Having arrived at about one o'clock we sat and ate our special lunch in the car looking over the stunningly beautiful landscape of mountains and valleys and little houses dotted in the distance. It was a cold but sunny day. Driving down the bumpy farm track, we recognised some of the dogs we had seen during the summer and as we approached the yard, we were met by a black and white collie who wanted to play ball. This was the mother of the puppies we had come to see. The farmer and his wife were happy to meet us again and showed us the litter of puppies in the nearby stable. It was now up to us to choose the one we wanted so the girls after much discussion chose a puppy who seemed very friendly and wanted to play. We named him Spot, paid the farmer and started the journey home. At first, our new bundle of fun was very lively but our daughters made a fuss of him and settled him down where he fell asleep in their arms.

When we arrived home, we introduced Spot to our cat Misty. Spot chased Misty and tried to round him up! Misty was not going to have any of that and chased Spot, they had a great time. The girls decided that this was the best Christmas ever.

Their grandparents came round for Christmas tea, but my father was rather put out that they had not been invited to dinner and that we had gone on our journey to collect Spot.

The ecumenical healing services, which I had so passionately prayed for took place. They were advertised all over town and my mother invited me to the healing service at the main Methodist church in town, along with a friend of hers who had been suffering from severe migraine headaches for over twenty years. I had recently experienced more and more pain in my joints, which felt like arthritis. Several neighbours in the area were suffering similar health problems. I had learned to control the pain by removing dairy products from my diet. Unfortunately, the problem seemed to be getting worse and I was now in a lot of pain in all my joints.

We arrived at the church and were made to feel welcome. We enjoyed singing the hymns and listened to the readings and teaching. Then those in need of prayer, were invited to go out to the healing ministers for prayer. The vicar of the large Anglican church in town and a young woman laid hands on me and prayed. I could feel her shaking with nerves as she did this. When they had finished I thanked them and returned to my seat feeling no different.

Nothing could have prepared me the following morning for the transformation that I was to experience. I woke up and got out of bed as usual, bright and early to get my husband's breakfast, but something was missing. What was it? It was pain! The pain had all gone and I could not believe it. I told my husband and he was amazed.

As soon as my mother was up, I rang her and told her the good news. She was thrilled. A couple of days later her friend told her that she was free of headaches and she remained that way. We were all so thankful for God's healing in our lives.

One morning when I was reading the Bible, it felt as though the Lord gave me a warning about Jim, where it described someone who has been delivered from an evil spirit. Unfortunately because that man turned his back on God the evil spirit returned bringing seven more wicked than itself (Matt. Ch. 12 v 43–45).

Sure enough, Jim's drinking was slowly starting to become a problem once more. Sometimes I would break down and walk away from it all – go off for a walk on my own just to get away from his abuse. Although I was sure that his abusiveness was not just caused by alcohol but also due perhaps to the fact that his eldest sister Joan still rejected us as a family and would have nothing to do with us since his brother Simon had died. I was disappointed that the healing that Jim had received seemed to have little effect now. I thought that if only he made a proper commitment to Jesus and let Him come into his life completely, and lead him in his daily life perhaps he could enjoy a happier and more trouble-free existence.

As Spot grew up, we introduced him to our local dog training club where he socialised with other young dogs and learnt to be obedient. He became very well behaved and earned a certificate for his obedience awarded to Jill for her patient training. Not to be outdone Kate decided that she would like to take Spot to a more advanced class where she also picked up a certificate for achievement.

We were invited to bring Spot along to agility training at a nearby village. This was great fun. Spot became very good at walking the narrow plank of the up and over and loved jumping through tyres, running through the tunnels and doing the weavy poles. We had a great time training him. The only thing that spoilt it was the fact there were too many of us and he only needed one handler.

Misty our much-loved cat was very entertaining. He used to chase Spot round the lawn and then Spot used to chase him. They had great fun and were good friends. He had a habit of coming to the front door at our house and somehow knocking the door as the letterbox and door knocker was quite low. One evening he did this, we opened the door, and in he walked with his girlfriend!

More recently though he had started to display some rather worrying changes to his character. He messed in the house a few times, which was not like him at all. He also seemed to have some funny turns. I did not think much of this until afterward when I realised that the poor cat had been badly affected by the nearby crop spraying. I had spoken to a friend who was experiencing similar problems with spraying near her house and she told me how her cat had gone blind and eventually died from this pollution.

I returned from a Christian meeting at the Methodist church in town. It had been very interesting and was about how originally doctor's careers in our country were grounded in the Christian faith.

The following day Misty was missing. We called and called him but he was nowhere to be seen. We continued to look for him the following day until Jim came home with him. He had been sadly knocked over by a car and had died. We were all devastated, as we loved him so much. We buried him in the garden and said some prayers for him. Spot missed him very much and seemed subdued and sad. This sad loss was very painful to me. I felt that I could not come to terms with it at all. I was convinced that this was not what God wanted. The hit and run driver who had knocked him over was probably speeding down our road as so many motorists seemed to do, as it seemed to be a short cut.

Eventually I felt Christ's reassurance that Misty was safe with Him in Heaven and then I could move on once again in my life. I was very thankful for my faith and although it was only a cat I mourned, I felt sorry at that time for those who had no faith and the terrible inconsolable loss they must feel when they lose someone they love.

After a while, we decided to have a kitten to replace Misty and were invited to an organic farm about ten miles away where there were several kittens looking for good homes. We went along and they were all so sweet, we did not know which one to choose. We decided on a beautiful long-haired tabby kitten. We brought him home and named him Sammy. Spot took to him straight away and he soon became a happy member of the family. He was very playful.

As summer returned so did Kate's health problems. It was suggested by the doctor at the hospital that animal fur could be a problem along with house dust. We decorated and spring cleaned her bedroom. We made the dog and cat comfortable outside in one of the outbuildings, but sadly this made no difference the health problem remained the same.

She steadily grew worse and I had more and more to adjust her diet once again to maintain better health and to reduce the asthma problem. I remembered what our next-door neighbour had told me one day that she could not go out during the summer months into her garden or she suffered with unbearable hay fever-like symptoms.

Poor Kate had yet another chest infection and was confined to bed. I went upstairs to see how she was and panicked because she had fallen asleep sitting up and her skin was an unhealthy grey blue colour. I panicked and thought I had lost her. I managed to wake her and called the doctor immediately. He told me to check her pulse and I gave him the reading. It was abnormally fast about twice as fast as it should be. He came out and gave her antibiotics again. This time however, after she had taken them she began to shake violently and she complained of double vision. I was so concerned for her. I prayed for guidance and felt that I should look at other ways of helping her.

I decided to look for an alternative health treatment for Kate as we were getting nowhere with our G.P. or the hospital. I contacted the same acupuncturist who had treated Jim nine years previously.

Unfortunately, he had now retired but his daughter was now doing the same work. I booked Kate in for an appointment.

When we arrived at the clinic, I introduced Kate to the acupuncturist Claire. Kate was a little scared about the prospect of the acupuncture needles. Claire gently explained that the treatment would not hurt but it would help her. During the first treatment to ascertain what was wrong she had a violent reaction and was sick. This did not deter the acupuncture doctor who discovered health problems that she was suffering with, and the best way to treat her for her condition. She found that Kate was suffering from Candida Albicans through all the antibiotics she had received and said that she needed to go on a special diet to eliminate this. We booked in for another appointment and she started a course of treatment.

One day while I was waiting for Kate to have her treatment, I picked up a magazine in the clinic and began to read it. Nothing could have prepared me for what I read. I noticed an article about crop spraying and read this with interest. Most of the symptoms described in this article were identical to those that Kate was experiencing. Then I remembered the tractors and the spraying equipment that regularly drove past our house in the summer months. It started to dawn on me that this was what was damaging Kate's health but also my husband, our other daughter and I had been experiencing some odd symptoms recently. Reading this article it all tied in. I told Claire. Her first reaction was that we should think about moving.

On the way home, I thought about Jim's abusive behaviour. Mental disturbance apparently was one of the symptoms of this chemical interference into the unfortunate people's lives who lived nearby to where crops are sprayed so the magazine had said.

When my husband returned home from work that evening I told him about the day's events. He was not impressed at all about the possibility of moving. He had recently completed work on a beautiful new kitchen and bathroom for us. He said that if we could prove that it really was crop spraying that was causing our health problems that he would think about moving.

I contacted a support organisation for those who had been damaged by crop spraying. They gave me the name and telephone number of an environmental specialist who only treated people privately. I thought to myself that this is going to be expensive. His practice was about thirty miles away but we made an appointment and he examined Kate, checked her for allergies and arranged for her to have some special blood tests done, not available at our local hospital. He told us that if we really were suffering from pesticide poisoning that we should move house because it was like living next to a chemical factory and it could cause motor neurone disease.

I took her to London for the blood tests. She hated needles and injections and made a big fuss about it. The test results sent to us confirmed that she was suffering multiple chemical poisonings. My husband was still very reluctant to sell the house. As the summer months continued Kate was now so ill that she came out in eczema all over her legs so severely that they had to be bandaged every night. She was also suffering with confusion and blurred vision, which was affecting her schoolwork.

Desperate to protect her health I took her to a Homeopathic Doctor for treatment. This worked well with the acupuncture treatment. I had to take on three jobs to pay for all this private treatment. The long hours in the multiple jobs were taking their toll and I was becoming very tired.

CHAPTER 8

The way forward in God's care

One Sunday morning I woke up and felt led by the Holy Spirit to go to the Pentecostal church in the city where we had lived. We had often attended this church together as a family. I drove over and was warmly welcomed. Just after the worship, someone got up and spoke in tongues. Immediately afterwards the lady sitting next to me stood up and translated this into English. It really sounded as though this was meant for me. I was amazed as she said that Jesus was looking after this person and that they were about to walk through some troubling times through brambles and nettles, but that He would lead them and bring them to a place of safety. I felt very moved by this word and returned home after the service with a wonderful peace.

I could no longer work with my oil paints as they were making me ill. I assumed that this was because I had been poisoned with the chemicals used in crop spraying in the nearby fields. Due to other debilitating health problems, as well I was finding it increasingly difficult to go out to work, and really needed to be able to work from home. I prayed about this and wondered what work I was going to do now. I felt that Jesus was encouraging me to turn to my piano and wondered if I could perhaps teach others in the same way that I had taught my two daughters to learn to play the piano. Recently we had bought Kate a keyboard for her birthday and I wondered if she would mind if I used it to teach this to pupils as well. I started to advertise and it was not long before I had several pupils to teach. I was quite nervous about teaching other people to start with, but my confidence grew as I handed it more and more over in prayer.

We decided it would be nice to have a holiday abroad as a family. We booked a holiday in Spain to travel by coach and stayed in a caravan at the other end. We had a lovely time and it was wonderful to see Kate enjoying herself after all the suffering she had gone through. The glorious sunny weather and relaxing holiday seemed a million miles away from the difficulties we were experiencing at home, but I thought it was too good to be true and then Jim's drinking once again spoilt everything. He was very irresponsible when he had too much to drink. He embarrassed us as a family and was so drunk one night that he did not lock up the caravan when he came in and left the door wide open all night. Anyone could have walked in during the night and harmed our daughters or stolen our belongings and money. I was shocked and horrified at his denial the following morning that there was anything wrong.

When we returned home, eventually my husband decided that we had better move. We put the house up for sale and while others around us were taking a year or more to sell their homes, we sold ours in one week to a cash buyer. We could not believe it but I knew that nothing is impossible with God. We searched around for another home in the town and became tired of searching through house details given to us by the estate agents. We decided to drive round instead and look at areas where we thought we would like to settle. This was a good course of action because we found an estate in the middle of town, which was a cul-de-sac and was so quiet that it felt more rural than the home we were selling. The only down side to this was that the garden was a lot smaller.

A few weeks after we had moved into our new quiet town home Kate's eczema vanished and all the food allergies that she had developed since living in the countryside just disappeared! She looked so much healthier. She was able to put weight on again, which she certainly needed to do.

During the winter months, I took Jill and Kate to a nearby riding school as they loved horses and kept pestering me to take them. They were in their element, but sometimes had a mild reaction when they came into contact with ponies. Although we had found a school where the ponies were really well groomed and as long as they wore gloves they seemed fine. We found through trial and error that if my daughters and I went on to a vegetarian diet which included fish but was dairy free that they had no reaction to the horses when they went riding at all which was quite amazing, but they did not remain on this diet.

Spring had arrived once more and we decided to have some fun so we booked a day trip on a Welsh farm for trail riding and pony trekking in Wales. Our oldest daughter felt quite confident so she went with the more advanced team, while the rest of us took a slow ride until lunch time. My husband, who was not interested in trying out the vegetarian diet, broke out in an awful eczema rash after about two hours. Although he had ridden before he had never had any problems like this. I felt so sorry for him and it spoiled his day and ours. He quickly recovered when he was out of that environment and on the coach home.

As the summer drew to an end, we decided that we would like a horse on loan for the winter, from the farm in Wales and we were able to go and select him. His name was Tom and he was a twelve-year-old piebald. The girls and I agreed to share the task of caring for him. We found grazing and a stable about a mile away. Fortunately, we all had bikes and could go and feed him and attend to him easily. The winter became very cold and wet and his field turned to a muddy quagmire. We kept him in the stable for a while but one day I discovered that the livery yard owner was removing him and putting other horses into his stable. As I had bought and put down the straw and placed his hay in his stable, I thought that this was unfair. I had a friend who lived about five miles away and had her own horses, stables and fields so I rang and asked if she had space for Tom for the rest of the winter. She agreed and we had him moved there. He was a lot happier, had plenty of space to roam around and a nice field and stable if he needed it. I had to go over in the car now to feed him but I did not mind. Our daughters used to go over at the weekends to ride him round the nearby quiet villages.

Jim could not do much gardening at our new home but he did start a neighbourhood watch for our estate. He tirelessly walked round and knocked on every door to set this up, organising meetings for our neighbours with the police to make sure our estate became more secure.

I continued with my piano and keyboard teaching and continued to advertise until I had a large number of pupils coming for lessons each week to our home.

Our cat Sammy had suffered an ongoing sight problem brought on we believed by the pesticides that he had been exposed to where we had lived. Our vet did not understand and blamed us and said that his diet was deficient and we needed to give him taurine tablets. This really upset me and it did not seem to make sense as I had always fed him a good diet the same as Misty had. Our vets seemed very money-orientated now and seemed to be expensive to visit. They were a far cry from the vets where I had worked before I was married, who were really caring people. Sammy seemed to manage to cope with the neighbourhood and feel his way around the different steps and areas that he toured regularly.

Both our daughters were now at the senior school and seemed to be happy and doing well.

My father called me up one day and asked me to go over because he was worried about my mum. I dropped everything and went over to see how she was. She apparently suffered bad headaches for several days and now seemed semi-delirious and confused. About ten minutes after I had arrived she collapsed and had convulsions. I was very shocked but tried to make sure that she was laying the right way and did not come to any harm with what limited first aid knowledge I had. My father called for an ambulance. They were a little slow coming and needed a second call to see how long there were going to be. When they arrived, they did their best for my mum and when she arrived at hospital, she was put into a side ward on her own and given many tests to find out exactly what was wrong. Apparently, she had suffered from a stroke. They found that her blood pressure was high and that she had become diabetic. I could not believe what had happened and kept praying for her.

When I visited her the next day she seemed a little better. The doctor had told her that she needed complete rest. It was a worrying time, but she received lots of prayer and slowly recovered. After she arrived home, she was upset that she could not do anything, and although I did my best to make sure she had some reading she became bored and started to get up and do a few things. She had a relapse and was re-admitted into hospital.

When mum was sent home the second time, I insisted that she stay in bed and have complete bed rest, with a small amount of necessary exercise for a week, then just get up for a few hours each day. I felt led to insist on these instructions after praying for her and receiving answers for her wellbeing.

I cancelled all my piano and keyboard pupils for a while and continued to help look after my mother. Slowly she recovered and started to look and sound more her own self.

Eventually I took her to the same hospital dietitian that Kate had received help from years previously. She was very helpful in sorting out a good diet for my mum for the diabetes that she was now suffering from which could be controlled successfully with diet.

Eventually my mum got stronger and fully recovered.

Jill had a glowing report and at open evening, her teachers told us how well she was doing.

A year later Jill sat her GCSE exams and we were surprised that she did not achieve better grades. She was undecided about what career she wanted to do but agreed to go to the college at a nearby town and study A level music and art and see if she could achieve a better grade in her maths.

After Jill left school Kate started experiencing more bullying from children of teachers who should have known better. Her life was made a misery and she was often very upset. It became difficult to go to church on a Sunday with our daughters because the teachers and their children who were doing the bullying were there also. Despite my complaining to the school, the situation remained the same.

As our daughters reached their mid-teens, they changed dramatically. Friends just said that this is what teenagers are like, but although I know that I was not perfect at that age, as I used to lose my temper sometimes and my room was untidy, what they went through was a complete nightmare.

We always encouraged them if they went out, to go out in a party of three or more for safety. This worked well for our eldest daughter until she left school and went to college at the age of sixteen and unfortunately got into a bad crowd, started smoking, became introvert and very difficult. She did not want to converse with her parents.

She would go off to college in freezing temperatures with soaking wet hair, that she washed and styled in curls, her room was a complete dump and she wore black all the time and played heavy metal music.

At school, she had been very conscientious but now she started to neglect her work as her musical and artistic gifts became more and more wasted.

Our younger daughter also started smoking. She was repeatedly bullied at school and the teachers did nothing to rectify the situation as the bullies were teacher's children. I could not believe what was going on in the Christian school that she was attending. In her last year at school, her class had three maths teachers and one of them had suffered with a nervous breakdown. Understandably, through all the problems Kate was suffering at school, her education was affected and she seemed to have a large chip on her shoulder. I prayed daily for the situation that Kate was in and did my utmost to put a stop to the bullying, but it persisted. She asked me in her final year if she could change schools to a private school as nothing could be worse than the school where she was. Sadly, we could not afford to do this and even if we could, she was already half way through her final year.

When Jill left college she had achieved an A level in art, failed her music and a low GCSE math's grade.

She went straight into a warehouse to work and sadly seemed satisfied with this. She did not receive very good treatment where she worked but stood up for herself to a certain extent and put up with it.

Her sister left school with disappointing exam results, possibly due to the way she had been treated at school. She also went straight into warehouse work.

Soon afterwards, she met a boyfriend who seemed a bit unstable and we were trying to protect her by insisting she return home at a reasonable time when she went out. She threatened to leave home and ran away to a nearby Youth Club, which was a place where homeless young people and drug takers frequented. We managed to find her and bring her home again. We tried reasoning with her but she was very volatile. One day when she was in one of her hostile tantrums, she scratched my arm with her nails the full length. I could not believe what was happening to our children.

We had an invitation to go to tea at my parents' home. While we were there I was chatting to my father, I think that Jim and our daughters were playing outside. I mentioned to him about the moral decline of our society. I was shocked at his attitude, he seemed amused.

Realising that my youngest daughter was disturbed I persuaded her to come with Jim and myself for healing at a Christian Healing Centre about twenty-five miles away. Thankfully, she agreed to go and we all went along to the meeting at the Centre one Friday evening. During the meeting, we were all prayed for in turn. When my turn came, the healing minister praying for me told me that the Lord was telling her that it was as though there was a spider's web wrapped around us as a family, round and round and round. She broke it and unravelled it in the Name of Jesus. She confirmed that it was witchcraft. I was shocked and disturbed by this revelation but I knew that there was something wrong because as a family we had been experiencing so many difficulties. I hoped that now our lives might improve.

Kate became increasingly more and more frustrated working in the warehouse. She applied for some office jobs, but because she had no qualifications for this work, this did not help. Eventually she received a job at an engineering company in the accounts department and shown the work she was to do. She slowly progressed and became more competent in her work, but her supervisor was very unreasonable, bullied her and made her life miserable. After almost a year of bad treatment, she left because she was so unhappy. We did our best to support and encourage Kate. Her next office job involved her running the whole office for a catering company. She worked so hard and turned the company round for them as it was failing and drummed up trade. It was an enormous responsibility for one so young, but helped us all to see what she was made of. Her wage was very low and her employers ungrateful. She was made redundant after three months because they did not want to pay the agency the large fee that they would have charged for supplying them with a permanent employee.

My piano and keyboard tuition was becoming undermined with the advent of a new music teaching programme at our local college on Saturday mornings. These lessons were held in classes without individual guidance. Although my fees for teaching on a one-to-one basis were reasonable, theirs were less and the number of my pupils became less. I was also noticing that many of my pupils lacked commitment and were more interested in playing on their computers than doing their piano and keyboard practise. I enrolled myself on to a word processing computer course at another local college and applied for secretarial positions. Eventually, I received a full-time sales office secretarial job and gave up my teaching, as the two jobs combined would have been too much. I settled into the job reasonably well but found that the secretary I shared the office with was a little resentful of my presence. I found that some of my work on my computer had been sabotaged by her, which was upsetting. I persevered and eventually we were able to get on reasonably well together. The company moved premises and started to really thrive. At this point, they started to get involved in working with a large organisation and were sub-contracted to work with nuclear energy. They had delivered to their premises equipment involved with the nuclear fuel industry, which was stored and worked on in their factory. As I was unaware of the extent of what was going on I continued as part of my job to deliver paperwork to the management in the factory.

It was not long before I started to have some very unpleasant health problems develop. I went to the doctor who told me that I had a fibroid the size of a melon and needed a hysterectomy operation. I was in a lot of pain and suffering from a lot of regular blood loss. I felt completely washed out. From home, I rang my employers to explain what the doctor had said. Later that day they rang me back to tell me that I no longer had a job to go to as it would take three months for me to recover from the major operation that I needed and they were not prepared to wait for my recovery. I had now worked for this company for over a year and had done a lot of work for the managing director and his directors to a high standard. I felt very let down. I handed all this over to the Lord, as there was nothing I could do about it. We were now without my earnings and would soon be struggling financially. Added to the misery my doctor now told me I would have to wait three months for the operation as their funding was being stretched.

A few nights later, I suddenly lost a lot of blood and nearly collapsed. I was rushed to hospital where one of the nurses that greeted me was a Christian friend. She assured me that she would have a word with Dr Bright the surgeon to try to bring my much-needed operation further forward. I returned home after being told by the doctor to have complete bed rest and not even to read as I was suffering with anaemia. My husband and family seemed resentful that I was no longer able to look after them and that they had to look after me!

A week later, I rang the other gynaecology surgeon Dr Downing at the hospital to see if he could help me any quicker. He offered to see me privately, so I made an appointment for a further examination. This was costly and we had to use savings we could not really afford.

A few days later Dr. Bright contacted me and said he could do the operation on the N.H.S. in five days time. I could not believe this good news, and praised the Lord. Many Christians who had heard of my plight were praying for me at this point.

I fasted for the required time and the day of the operation came. I woke up and found I was suffering from a further large blood loss. I was fearful in case the surgeon would refuse to carry out the operation. My husband came with me to the hospital and stayed with me until I was taken into the operating theatre. I really appreciated this. I was feeling very weak by now. When I came to, I was receiving a blood transfusion and had needed three pints of blood. I was totally dependent on the medical staff for everything I needed. They were the most kind and caring nurses that anyone could have wished for to care for them. They had a good sense of humour and made us laugh (although it hurt!). I made friends with some lovely people who were on my ward. One in particular was a teacher at a prominent grammar school in our town. She had a very interesting story to tell me about her son.

He had gone a similar way to my children and although he had been given every opportunity to do really well at school, he just could not be asked to put the effort into it. Consequently, he ended up in a dead-end job and she and her husband who was also a teacher were quite upset about this, but she did have a good sense of humour, which rubbed off on to me. The compassion shown by the nurses and the sister in particular to me had me in tears and I was able to share how my husband and family were treating me. She gave me some helpful advice, which stood me in good stead for when I returned home and made me feel as though I should have more self-worth.

I returned home to a clean and tidy home but this was not to last. I needed regular baths to aid the healing of the wound. I could not bend over to clean the bath myself so relied on my family to do this for me. The good will became less and less.

A week later, the nurse came once again to check everything was healing all right and she was alarmed to find that I was suffering from an abscess on the wound. She called the doctor who immediately had me returned to hospital for treatment and rest. Eventually I returned home once more.

I was ordered by my doctor to rest and he said that I might be well enough to return to working within six weeks of having the operation.

Six weeks after I had the operation I felt fit enough to go camping with my husband and our dog and we were able to do some walking in beautiful countryside. We found a quiet site at the foot of some spectacular rugged hills where there were not too many other campers. We had some lovely walks and one morning decided to do a longer walk along the hilltops that day. We got lost and eventually found our way back down a 'goat track', which was a bit dangerous and steep, but we managed. It was a hot day and we were all glad to get back to the tent. We had walked about twelve miles and I was amazed that I had been able to do this and thanked God for his healing power. As we returned home from that holiday two days later a thunderstorm followed us all the way back.

Meanwhile back at home our youngest daughter was starting to give us a great deal of worry. She had decided that she was going to leave home and went to live in a shared house with several other young people who had problematic lifestyles and some of which took drugs. She managed to find herself another job in a nearby warehouse on the evening shift, which involved walking down a dark country lane late at night on her own. This made us feel anxious. She did not want to listen to anything we said to her any more so we just had to let go and let God protect her. She was involved with a boyfriend living at this shared house and eventually became torn between him and another young man at the house who she fell in love with.

Eventually she returned home but now she thought nothing of dabbling in drugs, going to house music concerts and drinking heavily. She and her sister often went out for a drink and became so drunk that Kate vomited everywhere, and they became unwelcome in some places. They used to treat me with contempt. Their father was working nights and did not see everything that was happening. Regularly they walked through our home deliberately with muddy feet straight across the lounge carpet to their rooms. They thought it was hilarious when their father used to hide drinks under the car because he did not want me to know how much he was drinking.

Devastatingly both our daughters were arrested Jill when she was with her boyfriend in a nearby town and Kate when she got involved in a fight which was going on in the middle of town and she tried to stop it, but got involved. Through this, the police told her that she would have to testify in court against a very rough character and she had a police record, which made it even more difficult for her to get a good job. Both daughters had no respect for the police, or the church or anyone who attended it.

I was given a temp job as secretary at a design company. I was only there for a couple of weeks. I noticed that I was having some problems with my eyes. They felt sore and gravely and were red and bloodshot. I bought myself some eye drops from the chemist and it seemed to clear up. I continued temping as I searched for a permanent job, but increasingly found that I kept suffering with eye infections. Eventually I received a part-time receptionist position. I settled into this work and enjoyed what I was doing.

My eye problems got worse. I went to the doctor who referred me to an eye specialist. I also had my eyes tested. The optician told me that the HRT that I was taking following my hysterectomy operation might be causing dry eye. The specialist could not find anything wrong with my eyes. I was beginning to think that maybe the computer screen was causing the problem although I had worked full time in front of a computer in the job I had before my operation. I told the specialist about my thoughts. She was very interested and said that she might find this useful for other patients.

When I was at work, I found the symptoms were worsening. My eyes were very bloodshot, my heart raced, my joints ached, and I suffered severe headaches down one side of my head. My boss realised that I was not well and suddenly and unexpectedly made me redundant, doing away with the receptionist job and calling other members of staff to take it is turns to man the reception area. I stopped taking the HRT in case it was causing the problem, and felt a little better. I was now reluctant to work in an office in case the same thing happened again. I applied for a warehouse job where there were not computers everywhere. Although monotonous, I enjoyed working in the warehouse as I and other members of staff there often had a good laugh.

It was not demanding and I could plan other things while I did this repetitive work. About a year later, however, I had become increasingly sensitised to computer screens, microwaves and mobile phones. I was shocked that the electromagnetic fields emitted by the computer screens at the far end of the warehouse were at last affecting me. My employers were sympathetic, but I realised that I had to leave.

My doctor did not really understand the problem and was unable to help me apart from offer some anti-allergen tablets and suggest that maybe my stem cells had been damaged in some way. She signed me off and I was given incapacity benefit.

CHAPTER 9

The truth revealed

I felt great sadness as my family's Christian faith deteriorated with increasing problems thrown at them mainly attributable through witchcraft with abnormal regularity, as careers were repeatedly destroyed and with ongoing health problems due to severe stress.

All I could do was repeatedly watch them take the wrong road in their lives further contributing to their misery as they walked further and further away from the Lord who was waiting to help them but I continued to pray for them.

I spoke to a Christian friend of the family, whose daughter was at school with our daughters. She seemed to understand that what we were experiencing was abnormal, and completely unexpectedly, she said, "It is your father who is causing all these problems" as though the Holy Spirit had given her that insight.

I went to my doctor to see if she could help me with my health problems but also I was concerned about my youngest daughter who was having problems with stunted hair growth on the crown of her head and emotional problems causing her to become anorexic. Unfortunately, my doctor did not have the time to help me and was unkind and unhelpful.

Soon after this, I broke down and felt that I really needed help to carry on. My doctor had struck me off because she did not understand my health problems. I prayerfully looked through the Yellow Pages to look for a psychotherapist and booked an appointment. This man was very helpful. He showed me how I needed a complete change of plan in my life. How

I needed to let my adult children go and how worrying about them would not help in any way. He also said that his wife had experienced similar problems in letting their son go who also had various problems. It all sounded so easy, but I continued with the programme and a couple of months later I felt a new person. This was just what I needed and I was very grateful for the help I received.

I changed my doctor and the first time I went to the new practice I was seen by a doctor who was very unpleasant. He told me that I was imagining the pain and symptoms I was experiencing when I came into contact with computer screens, mobile phones and microwaves and that I needed to see a psychologist. I was furious at his undermining attitude towards me. If I needed to see a doctor now I had to wait outside until the doctor was ready to see me because of the possible pollution that might threaten me in the waiting room.

Even Christian friends had been alienated towards us in a strange way. A very good Christian friend in the next town where we had lived fell out with me through a witchcraft related problem that I was completely ignorant about at the time.

Then I received a frightening revelation while I was minding my parents' bungalow in August 1998, as they were on holiday. My father had a difference of opinion with me over my adult children and was angry with me because I did not agree with him. As I was watering the plants and tidying up in the kitchen, I bent down to pick something up. My back felt as though it had been stabbed with a knife and the pain was horrendous. I managed to stand up again with great difficulty, limp back to the car and return home. I was laid up for a week with a bad back. When I prayed for an answer as to why I was in such pain and what on earth I had done, the Lord brought back to me the resentfulness that my father had towards me just before he and my mother went away on holiday. It seemed as though He was telling me that my father had inflicted this terrible back pain on me as a punishment. Then the Lord went on to show me many other warnings of danger that my family, I and even my mother was in, from my father who was practicing witchcraft. I really did not want to believe this. It was like a sinister fairy tale from which I wanted to escape. I repeatedly asked the Lord for guidance on this because I wanted to understand what He was telling me correctly.

I wrote many lists of all the things the Lord was telling me that my father was attempting to do to us as a family, but also to others. I was horrified and disgusted with my father. The only way I knew how to deal with this was to say the deliverance healing prayers Rev. Long had taught me several years before. This took up several hours each day.

The Lord had warned me about two years previously that my mother was growing very tired of all the problems she and we were experiencing in our lives and felt as though she no longer wanted to carry on. I felt the Lord telling me again that the time was fast approaching when she would be going to her Heavenly home.

I searched for the help of other Christians who would understand and be able to pray about this situation. I found a couple in a village in the Cotswolds who specialised in deliverance healing. I visited them and spent some time explaining the situation to them. I asked them what I could do, and how I could pray to prevent my father from harming us as a family any more. Sadly, they told me that there was nothing that I could do, except forgive my father and pray for him. They spent some time praying for my family, my father and myself. I left and drove home but still felt worried about the situation.

It was early December. My mother rang to tell me that she was suffering with flu symptoms and a headache. I said that I was sorry that she was not well and that I hoped that she would soon be feeling a lot better. She told me not to visit her in case I caught it.

Not thinking a great deal of this I continued with my preparations for Christmas. I always made my own Christmas pudding, Christmas cake, mince pies, chocolate log and pickles. It was like a family tradition. My mum always did the same. This year as well I made some extra goodies for Jim's dad, as he was now over eighty and struggling to do things for himself so much. Added to this there was also my family to think of. It was a very busy time. A few days later, I rang my mum to see if she was any better. She said that she still felt unwell but was looking after herself and was not going out. My father was doing the shopping and looking after things.

Several more days went by and my father rang. He sounded very upset and said that my mum had been taken ill and had suffered another stroke. He apparently had just returned from doing some shopping and she keeled over as she was giving him a cup of tea. She had been taken to hospital and this was where he was ringing from. He asked me to go straight to the hospital. I was in the middle of shampooing our lounge carpet, because our daughters had repeatedly walked into the house without wiping their shoes and the carpet looked dirty. I quickly finished what I was doing, and went to the hospital.

When I arrived, my father said the doctor had told him, that my mother would not recover from this stroke and that her body was shutting down, as she was in a coma. Inwardly I was very upset but I tried to be strong for my father. I hoped that the doctor was wrong but feared that this was it, the warning that the Lord had given me. I felt bad that I had not gone over to see my mum when she said that she was not feeling well. I went in to see her in the single ward where she was. She was breathing erratically and she was unconscious. I held her hand, squeezed it, and hoped that she understood that I was there. I prayed for her not to suffer and if it was the time for her to go to be with the Lord that He would take her without suffering.

A doctor walked into the room to see how she was. He told us there was nothing that he could do and that her body was shutting down. I thought that this was a little insensitive in front of my mother, even though she was unconscious. After he left the room, I saw that she had shed some tears. Perhaps she could hear what was happening but could not respond. This was very sad. As she passed away, I felt very emotional and tearfully kissed her before we left.

This was the moment I was dreading. I now had to take my father back to our home, as I could not expect him to go back to his lonely bungalow. Our eldest daughter gave up her bedroom for my father and she slept on the settee.

When my mother passed on I felt led to fast for her for several days and then eventually had a reassurance that she had safely reached Heaven. Before that, however, I felt the Lord telling me that my still born sister was wandering around as a lost soul and my mother was torn as to whether to stay with her or to go up to Heaven. I have since prayed for her and feel that she is now in Heaven with my mother.

I went with my father to register the death and organise the funeral. As I was suffering from sensitivities to computers and mobile phones, I was restricted as to where I could go. My father had to go into the Registrar's office himself. It was Christmas time and the funeral was delayed, because of the holiday period and could not be held for three weeks. This made the situation a lot worse.

My father was like a lost soul. The atmosphere at our home was very fraught. Our youngest daughter had an eating disorder and was losing weight fast, whilst our eldest daughter was piling the weight on. I was worried about Kate and did all I could to encourage her to eat. Nothing was working. I continued to pray for her. Then I believe that the Lord gave me an idea, to use a diet sheet for loss of weight and reverse it. I started making goodies that even she could not resist loaded with fat! Her health suddenly started to get a lot worse, suffering with eczema as bad as when we lived at our last house. I was very concerned about her wellbeing and thought that my father may have something to do with this. I became very angry with my father and very concerned about my family while he was staying with us. I tried ringing Rev. Long who had now become Bishop Long and was in London, hoping that he would be able to pray for the situation. He was too busy to help me and said that I should be able to pray about this situation myself, but if I really needed help to contact his friend a minister in Birmingham. I experienced flashbacks of relatives and friends who had died suddenly and unexpectedly. Perhaps they were the victims of my father's witchcraft. I felt fear and panic. I straight away contacted this minister and asked if I could come and speak to him. He arranged for me to go and see him the following week. I felt very relieved.

My sister-in-law Valerie rang us and spoke for some time. It was good to hear from her. I sensed that my father resented this.

My Father had stayed with us for a week now and I was feeling that if he did not go home soon, perhaps he never would. I did my best to help him and reassure him. He returned to his home and I arranged to go and see him regularly to make sure he was all right, but I was determined that he look after himself and not expect me to do everything for him. A friend of my mother offered to cook him meals, which I thought was unnecessary, as he was quite able to look after himself. He was invited to visit another of my mother's friends, which was nice for him to get out and have a change.

I went to see the minister in Birmingham and told him about the witchcraft that had come down my father's family line and of how I believed that he was using this on us and other people as well. I said that I did not know how to deal with the situation and asked if he could help and that Bishop Long had recommended that I contact him. Rev. Harding prayed with me for a short time and then I left. He also told me that there was little I could do while my father was practising witchcraft against us.

My family continued to seem to be suffering and I wondered if it was through my father staying with us. One night while I was lying in bed, I sensed an evil presence next to the bed and then it felt as though a heavy weight was on top of me. I panicked and prayed to God for protection and deliverance of whatever it was. I prayed that I might be free of the burden of this problem and that my father would pass on, if this was God's will. Little did I know the problems that would follow if this happened.

About a week later I had a phone call from my father's neighbour who lived across the road. It was mid-morning and usually my father was up and about there was probably no need to worry but the curtains were still closed at his home. I tried ringing, but there was no answer. I rushed over to the house and knocked the door. Once again, there was no answer. I asked my father's next-door neighbour for his help and he suggested that we ring the police and they break in to see if my father was all right.

The police came out immediately, broke the glass in the front door and entered the house. They found my father in his bedroom where he had passed away very suddenly. They tried to stop me going to look, because he had been in the middle of getting dressed, when he had suddenly been taken ill, keeled over and died. The gas fire was still on in the dining room with clothes he must have washed airing out round it on the clothes horse and the water was still in the sink in the bathroom where he had just had a wash.

Although I wanted rid of the horrendous problem of witchcraft, which had haunted me throughout much of my lifetime and had caused so many problems to my family, I was very upset that my father had died as he did, with no one there to be with him. He had died only five weeks after my mother. It was a terrible shock. The post mortem revealed that one of his main arteries going to his heart was damaged and he had lost a lot of blood very quickly.

I was stunned. I also felt inwardly relieved that he would no longer be able to practice witchcraft on us anymore. My husband was notified and he left work to comfort me. My cousins came round to offer me support as well. Before we left my father's home that day Jim my husband suggested that we take a few valuable items with us to make sure that they were safe. It was the last thing that I was interested in at the time, but I did as he suggested. As we picked the items up, I felt a deep foreboding and a real feeling of evil. We put these few things into the car and drove home. When we reached home, I realised that we had made a big mistake bringing these belongings with us, because they did not feel like mine, but my father's. It felt as though the Lord was warning me and telling me to return them to my father's home as soon as possible. I felt very uncomfortable and as though we were in some sort of danger. I returned these items the following day.

There was an awful lot of things that needed sorting out in my parents' home. When we looked in the loft, we found items that they must have kept throughout their married life. It was like walking into a time warp.

I contacted the minister once again from Birmingham hoping that he would come and bless my parent's home, as there was no priest or minister in our town that I felt I could ask. He said that he and his wife would be happy to come and pray through my parent's home.

The following week they arrived and spent about an hour praying at the home. They said that they felt some sort of battle had taken place on the site where the house was many years ago and that there were unsaved souls wandering about who they prayed for. God spoke to me, prior to this, warning me that these people should not be praying about the witchcraft, as they could be in danger of being harmed. He showed me that he wanted me to fast and pray about this situation myself. We held a communion service in the house. When they left, I felt peace and a relief.

I felt, however, that the Lord was instructing me to pray for my father's soul and for his brothers and sisters who had died. I went to the Catholic church near where we lived, lit candles for each one of them and during mass lifted up prayers for them all. I also went and prayed for my grandmother on my father's side and other relatives of his that I felt might need prayer.

Within a couple of days of doing this my sister-in-law Valerie, who I thought a lot of, suddenly died. She had been suffering from alcoholism, and liver damage amongst other things. This was a terrible shock to Jim and I and his remaining family, his father and sister. We had received so many bad shocks that we seemed to be on autopilot, when it came to us going to her flat, clearing it out and organising the funeral. We found that a church nearby where she lived had been taking an interest in her and encouraging her to go there. I was thankful of that because I had been praying for her for some time to come to the Lord. The minister was very kind, and encouraged us to organise the funeral however we liked. We did our best, but the terrible shock was taking its toll on us.

I spent about four months sorting out all the things in my parents' home giving things away to charity. I even had a market stall in a nearby town, and took items down to the tip. I lost count of the number of times I went there, as it was an endless job. I did this while Jim was at work and as I sorted through their belongings, I often had a cry. There were many unhappy as well as happy memories there. As I continued to sort everything out, I slowly made a decision that perhaps it might be best if we sold our home and moved into this one. After all my parents' home had a larger garden and the space inside the house was roughly the same as our own home, if we knocked two of the small rooms into one. After having the property valued in case we decided to sell it, we received a low valuation due to all the modernisation needed. At this point we decided to sell our home and have this place renovated and install new central heating, double glazing, a new kitchen and new wood work throughout because there was woodworm. We spent the next six months getting all this work done. There was not one job done satisfactorily though, as there was one problem after another with much of the alterations. The central heating system installed in a rush, gave us problems afterwards, the lock on the iron gates on the drive seized one day locking us in, the new guttering leaked and the kitchen installation was not finished off properly. Problems continued over many years at our new home. The dividing wall was knocked down and I stripped all the old wallpaper and replaced it with new emulsioning everywhere. I stained all the new woodwork and varnished it. At the same time, I was also redecorating some of the rooms in our home that needed it, and painting outside woodwork before we moved. Our next-door neighbour bought our house from us as an investment and gave us a fair price for it. Soon we were ready to move into our new home. By this time, I was feeling the effects of handling all these chemicals, from the emulsion paints, wood stain, gloss paint, and of course the wallpaper paste, varnish and turpentine. I started to have excruciating pains along my back, which seemed to be affecting by my digestive system. I was convinced that this was the result of pesticide poisoning twelve years previously and my body was still unable to cope with toxins very satisfactorily. I suffered with this for about three months. Eventually when I could stand the pain no longer, I went along to casualty at the local hospital, during the Christmas holiday and was given some tablets, which eased the condition. I then started to feel better.

The move into our new home was smooth and trouble free, as far as the solicitor and removal company were concerned. It felt strange at first, there were so many memories in this place.

My youngest daughter said that she felt uncomfortable here, as her grandfather had died here.

Nine months later, after I had to stop work due to sensitivities to modern technology, during which time I was receiving state sick pay, I was asked to go for an assessment at a special department at the job centre. Whilst there, the man that interviewed me asked me if I could sit, walk and stand I said yes. He then said that in that case I could go back to work. He had no understanding at all of my health problems.

In the meantime, my dentist suggested that I build up my immune system. At this suggestion, I obtained two books on the subject and did my best to do just that. I ate as much organic food as possible and tried to look after myself.

CHAPTER 10

My husband's difficulty with alcoholism

Winter was approaching when we moved into our bungalow, which we had refurbished. I was concerned about Sammy our long haired tabby cat settling down because his eyesight was so bad. After he had been kept inside for about ten days I let him out because he seemed distressed being kept in our home and wanted his freedom. Sadly, he wandered off and despite calling him and searching for him for weeks we never saw him again. Spot our dog missed him very much and seemed really down. About six months later, he had a heart attack and died. This was a sad time for us and we searched for a border collie puppy. It was not long before we were collecting Storm, a beautiful blue grey merle puppy, with blue eyes. He was very playful. I enjoyed taking him to dog training and for lots of walks, as he got older.

My husband was clearly becoming an alcoholic. He suffered with severe mood swings, causing many arguments between us. It did not help when he was encouraged by his friends to carry on drinking, even though he had started to go to AA and had cut right down on his drinking. After his friends gave him a good talking to – although it was his decision to go to AA – he said he was never going back again. Of course, I continued to attend my Al-Anon meetings for family members and friends of alcoholics, which I found very helpful.

I had to come to terms with the fact that I had allowed him over the years to eat away at my self-confidence, and undermine me so much that this was now having a serious effect on me. I realised I had to stop feeling sorry for myself and resolved that I would go out three evenings a week and possibly during the day on a Saturday and of course there was swimming on Sunday evening. I realised that I needed to stop being a people pleaser and live my life how I wanted to.

One Saturday I drove out to some beautiful gardens open to the public. It was a tranquil and blissfully quiet place. I drank in the colours of the flowers, shrubs and blossom from snowy white, to vibrant red and every conceivable pastel shade in between. There were numerous ponds, exotic ducks and geese that splashed about and called to each other. To round off my walk I treated myself to a cake and cup of tea in the tearooms. I planned to visit some more similar gardens, explore some nice quiet villages with tranquil walks, and do several hours walking each Saturday.

I also decided to contact some of my old friends and thought that perhaps we could go out for a meal or to the theatre. It was good to have a variety of interests and a life, which did not become boring or worse still revolve around my alcoholic family.

I was speaking to a neighbour down the road from us when he reminded me of how he had suffered breast cancer, as a result of aerial crop spraying. One of the chemicals that poisoned him was on the list of chemicals that had affected us when we were advised by our doctor to move house or the farmer's crop spraying nearby would kill us.

We were spring-cleaning and redecorating our home where it needed it. Jim decorated the kitchen and bathroom with low odour paint as the chemical allergy that I had now prevented me from doing this. I noticed the paint on the radiator had started peeling so suggested that he paint this as well with radiator paint.

I went and walked the dog while he sprayed the radiator. When I returned I could not believe the awful smell from this paint. I quickly rushed round the home and opened every window and the back door. I felt the chemical reaction kick in immediately and felt pain through all my joints.

Sadly, Jill split up with her boyfriend who she was buying a house with. She came back to live with us until the house was sold and she was able to buy a place of her own. She brought with her strong-smelling deodorants, liquid soaps and shampoos and insisted on using perfumed soap powder in our washing machine.

A couple of weeks later I started to react to these strong-smelling products and suddenly became so ill that I was forced to rest in bed for several days. I had to insist that all these products were removed from our home and that she used our soap powder, free from harsh chemicals. Poor girl she had to start to use plain naturally perfumed soap and shampoo. I found that I had become more chemically sensitive than I had been for some time. I repeatedly suffered with pain in my lower back if I came into contact with chemicals or strong perfume.

As I was sorting out the loft of the bungalow that my parents had left me when they died, I came across several things that seemed relevant to the troubles and persecution that we had suffered as a family. I found a comprehensive illustrated book about different schools throughout the UK and in particular public and private schools and grammar schools and even schools in Switzerland and Europe. This reminded me of the time my father had told me how he had done really well at school, and I could see this from his school reports, which were in a cupboard near the books on schools. He had been awarded mainly A's and a few B's for his work with excellent reports. He then went on to tell me that although he really wanted to go on to a local public school or the grammar school he knew that his mother could not afford this so he told her he did not want to continue with his education. Then I thought of what had happened to our daughters and then me and wondered if there was any significance in this.

Wednesday the following day, I felt very low. Jim had barely spoken to me for about a week. I was unsure why, apart from the fact that I said that I no longer wanted a pond in our garden anymore. We had planned this for a while and Jim slabbed the patio right up to where the pond was to go. Sadly, he had fallen into the dug-out pond, down a slope and a metre deep, once when he was drunk. I now had reservations about having a pond.

I suggested that we have a pebble fountain feature instead. We were also at cross purposes about our planned holiday to Hungary where we were supposed to be going to look for an area to buy a property to live. I had felt the need to leave our country due to a recently installed mobile phone mast only a few hundred feet from our home, that gave an intermittent signal straight through our home. The area where we lived had until recently been a quiet village but was now like a busy town due to the development of housing estates in only five years. We both agreed that it would be nice to live in a quiet rural area, where there was no crop spraying or mobile phone masts. We would be looking for a place set in beautiful countryside with woods nearby. All the countryside surrounding us for miles was prairie type fields full of crops that were regularly sprayed. Jim was also looking for an area near a river or lake where he could fish regularly. Apparently, Hungary fitted the bill.

Jim once again stormed out for a drink presumably with his friends but he never said where he was going anymore. I was feeling depressed this evening. It was raining but I did not care what the weather was doing. I went outside and weeded the back garden. It needed doing so desperately and it felt therapeutic. Jill asked me what I was doing. I told her that I just wanted to get the weeding finished. After I had finished the weeding Jill spent the evening with me. I had a good cry and explained to her that I was finding it hard work coping with her father. I told her that I was finding it difficult when she and her father go outside regularly for a smoke, because I could still remember how her father tried to turn her younger sister against me with numerous lies about me when they were outside smoking. I had overheard what he was saying when I innocently opened the front door to take in the free newspaper from the mailbox. She told me that she did not take sides, and that her father had not spoken ill of me in front of her. I found this hard to believe and went on to tell her a little more about her grandfather's sad upbringing and some of the things that I had found in the loft when I was sorting things out. I explained how her grandfather's mother had abandoned him and his sister when he was about thirteen years old. Their father was an alcoholic and so he decided to leave home, spending time at his half-brother's and his wife, which did not work out, and then he moved to another half-brother's home. He did not find out that they were not his full brothers until he was about fifteen years old and had to have his surname corrected to come into line with his birth certificate. I also told her about the strange coincidences of some of the upsetting things that happened to my father, that seemed to be mysteriously repeating themselves in our lives. I explained that I had been praying about the situation and would continue to do so until all the prayers were answered. She told me that she loves and cares about me and her dad. I now felt closer to Jill than I had for some time, which was a relief and a blessing.

Soon after our conversation Jill's dad returned smelling of alcohol. By now, Jim had been drinking every evening for about two weeks and he was adamant that he was never going to give up. He also said he wanted a divorce and he pulled off his wedding ring and threw it down next to our wedding photograph. He threatened that he would be going to the solicitors in the morning to arrange a divorce. I went to bed very upset and read two chapters of a Christian book, which really uplifted me. I prayed and went to sleep.

The next morning after Jill had gone to work Jim went out. I took the dog for a walk, did my cleaning and then waited for our internet provider to arrive to repair a fault. I felt drained and did not feel like doing much. The repair engineer arrived and did his best to sort out the fault. Jim arrived home and spoke to the engineer but would not acknowledge me. I felt that I needed something to cheer me up and rang the Ark of the Covenant church to ask if they had a healing mass that evening. Apparently, they had, so I decided to go to this and after dinner, I drove to the nearby city to attend it. I set off in plenty of time because it had become very popular. I was amazed at how quickly the little church filled up and recognized many friends there. Although small, this beautiful building had such a peaceful atmosphere. I could sense the Lord's presence and I was glad that I had come. The mass lasted two and a half hours and during this time Father John spoke as though led by the Holy Spirit words of comfort, strength and hope. He invited us to receive healing in many different areas of our lives as he spoke of the need to be able to forgive. I prayed for Jim and our marriage and when I left the church, I felt uplifted and joyful and as though I had received a further inner healing. I returned home on this note and told Jill of the lovely evening that I had enjoyed and invited her to come along if she wanted to another time. Jim spoke to me and asked me if I was all right. He had been drinking again though. I went to bed and slept peacefully.

The next morning, I was praying, when Jim came through to ask if we could talk. At first I thought oh no, because the 'talks' we had had recently were full of twisted truth and insults aimed at me. It seemed though today that there was some sort of change in Jim. I asked him if it could wait until I had finished what I was doing and had taken Jill to work as it was raining. He said OK but he felt a lot different today and wanted to tell me about how he felt. He said he was sorry and gave me a hug.

When I returned I sat down and listened to what Jim had to say. He said that he had woken up that morning feeling completely different and he really wanted to put things right and start again. He went on to say, that he had been to the solicitors yesterday but they did not have anyone who dealt with divorce in their office that day and recommended three other solicitors. As he visited the other solicitors, no one was able to help him. One that he contacted did not even deal with divorces. Jim then went to the Citizens Advice Bureau and they were closed! He said it seemed as though the Lord was blocking every direction he went in to find about divorce. We both agreed that we would try again. This time there seemed more tolerance and love between us.

A little later, the CRUSE counsellor knocked on the door for a further session with Jim. She was a very pleasant lady who had told him she was a Christian when he asked her if the cross that she was wearing was a fashion statement or if it meant more to her.

Later that day, after I had walked Storm our dog, and April the Counsellor had gone, Jim looked a bit confused. He told me that his head was in a spin and he needed to write things down because he could not believe what was happening. He mentioned that April had told him that she had been praying for him and that she and her husband had in the past both removed their wedding rings after rows, but everything had been put right afterwards. She also mentioned that she was a prayer minister at a local church. Jim was absolutely amazed at how God was working in his life!

The next day was our thirty-fourth wedding anniversary. We both gave each other cards and a big hug. We prayed together and thanked God that we were still together and were able to celebrate this day. We set off to go to my father-in-law's grave as it was his birthday the following day and on the way I said that I wanted to go to church to confessions. When we arrived at the church, I asked Jim if he would like to go to confessions as well. He declined but came into the church with me. After I had come out of the confession box and kneeled to pray, I asked him if he wanted to go now, but he refused and said that he would go to confessions after all. I was amazed. When he came back, he told me that he could not believe that he had just done that because he had made up his mind he was definitely not going to confessions today! If God is working in your life, many unexpected things can happen.

That evening we celebrated our wedding anniversary with a lovely meal together.

CHAPTER 11

The farewell barbeque

An Environmental Allergy Hospital, near London, did tests on me to find out what was causing the severe reactions I was experiencing to mobile phones, x ray equipment, large computer monitors and microwaves. Their findings confirmed that I did have a genuine reaction to these things and they even did electronic charts to show the reactions I was experiencing to this equipment and introduced me to many other patients also suffering with electromagnetic sensitivities. I was advised to sue my previous doctor who had insisted that I had a psychological problem, struck me off from his surgery, and left me without a doctor for several years. I complained to the surgery and to other NHS representatives including the Health Minister but it was a waste of time they just made up weak excuses. I gave up after a year of going round in circles and decided that I as a Christian did not want to sue a doctor. I was appalled at the attitude of some doctors and medical professionals in the NHS at this time.

It was late summer and I attended a farewell barbeque with friends, at a Christian Community in a nearby village, because they were leaving the area. They had done lots of valuable evangelization work and had been a real inspiration to me. I went along enjoying the lovely sunshine and a clear blue sky, after daily rain that lasted several weeks. I sat with some friends to eat. One of them asked me how my health was and I explained about my sensitivity to mobile phones, microwaves and x rays. To my surprise, David from our church understood and said that his daughter was dealing with radiation and its effects at the university where she worked. I explained about being poisoned by crop spraying and then ten years later I believed due to careless working conditions where I worked I had been affected by radiation from experimental work being carried out which then led to me needing major surgery. David and Rosemary insisted on praying for me and took me into the chapel. I felt I should be kneeling so I knelt down while Rosemary prayed in tongues and David was waiting on Jesus and the Holy Spirit to lead him how to pray. They spent about thirty minutes in prayer. I felt a real peace had descended on me and continued to enjoy the evening. The following day when I got up, I was amazed as I felt as though I had received a significant inner healing. The anxiety that I had about Jim had completely gone. It felt as though God was in charge of everything in my life. I felt a wonderful peace. I praised God for how he had transformed me.

The day after that was Sunday. Often on a Sunday evening, I went swimming. Up until this point, I was able to swim nearly a width before I had to stop to get my breath back, which took about five minutes, I was so lacking in energy. This particular Sunday when I went swimming, I found that I could continue swimming for about an hour without having to get my breath back. My energy levels had been transformed beyond belief! I was overjoyed and praised God for His healing.

The next day I went to our local supermarket for some groceries. As I reached the queue, the man in front of me began to use his mobile phone. Normally with my painful sensitivities, I would avoid people using mobile phones if I could because if I came into contact with them I would suffer severe reactions. These included pains in my head, bad effects on my eyes, my joints would ache and my heart would speed up considerably.

This time I decided to remain in the queue to see what happened. I was shocked because nothing happened. I continued to walk behind this man who was holding a conversation on his mobile and I had no reaction! I could not believe it. After all, I had suffered in this way for about eleven years. I came home and told my husband who was also amazed, and I do not think that he believed me.

That evening I went to 7 pm mass at church to say thank you. As I approached the entrance to the church a young woman was standing there using her mobile and I had to pass right next to her to go through the entrance. No reaction! I silently praised God once again and joyfully went into mass and gave thanks.

We flew to Hungary for a three-week holiday and landed at a small airport near Lake Balaton. We headed for an area, which is forested and is a national park conservation area. We stayed in a room of an Austrian-style chalet owned by the Hungarian forestry tourist board. It had a balcony where we could sit and watch endless varieties of birds coming and going through the trees. When evening came, some mysterious feathered visitors came and sat in the trees just out of our sight and started to converse. They sounded like large birds, but we do not know what they were. We also saw what looked like eagles soaring on the thermals high above the forest and calling to each other. It was a peaceful place where wildlife thrived. We made friends with the forest ranger and his girlfriend who had a cottage on the site where we stayed. He had two horses and was quite proficient at the national sport of archery on horseback. He invited us to watch him and we were impressed.

During our stay, we went to look at a fair one Saturday morning in the village. Our sense of smell led us to rows of cast iron cook pots over open fires containing Hungarian goulash. We discovered that this was a competition with a prize for the best recipe. There was an opportunity to try some archery, and many interesting stalls to look round. While we explored this beautiful area full of tall leafy trees and the appetising smells from the food that was cooking, we were approached by a colleague of our friend who knew we were looking for a home in Hungary. He invited us to go and look at his neighbour's home which was for sale. Cautiously we walked with him through the village until we reached the house, which looked quite large and stood on its own with mature trees and land surrounding it. He introduced us to the owner who seemed very pleasant. We were shown round this spacious five-bedroom house with two bathrooms and endless garage and cellar space built on a split-level. It was immaculate and my husband was impressed with the land that went with it. We wondered how much this property would cost and assumed that it would be above our budget. The owner welcomed us and invited to sit down on the patio and enjoy some homemade cakes and drinks. When we were told the price, we were shocked as it was only about a third of the value of our home in the UK, which was a much smaller property. We told the owner that we were interested in the property but would have to sell ours first.

Before we left Hungary to come home, we continued our search for homes and toured the southern part of the Country up to the Danube River. We found other beautiful areas and when we left for home, we were inspired.

As soon as we arrived home, we set to work organising the outside space to make our home look more attractive to sell. We transformed the front garden widening the drive, replacing the lawn with a gravel garden and retaining the colourful flower borders that surrounded it. We worked so hard that we managed to fill a large skip in three days! I organised a Cotswold stone sundial feature in the centre, which enhanced our front garden and gave more interest. We put our home on the market within three weeks of returning home from Hungary, as we did not want to miss the dream home that we had found. It was the beginning of October and two couples came to look at our home but then it went quiet.

I felt led to start working on an ecumenical Christian meeting to take place in our church hall each Friday. I was so thankful for the healing that I had received and looked forward to being able to share testimonies of how the Lord had healed and blessed me.

The meeting was to be open to all and was to include praise and worship, a talk by a speaker, prayers for healing, refreshments and Christian fellowship. We had the priest's blessing in what we were doing. I did not feel very confident about leading this meeting, as I did not have anyone to play the music for the worship songs. I decided to organise a special lead to connect my laptop and keyboard together and with the help of some special software on the computer proceeded to record the music we needed on to CDs. I also obtained an overhead projector that I could use with my laptop to put the words for the worship songs on to the wall for the people to see. I had a few teething problems with the recording of the music on to CDs, but managed to get it sorted out with some prayer.

When I prayed to Jesus, I was grateful for how He answered my prayers and soon we had a choice of many CDs to choose from and to sing to. I managed to find a selection of inspiring speakers and we had some wonderful answers to prayers for healing. This was very encouraging and we finished for Christmas with a special meeting and a Christmas party. We enjoyed our Christian fellowship together and no one wanted to go home!

Our estate agent suggested that we have an 'open day' and bring the price down on our home by £20,000. Wishing to sell as soon as possible, we agreed, but we were so disappointed that no one even came to the 'open day.' Just before Christmas we were notified by our friends in Hungary that the home we wanted to buy had been sold. We were devastated. We continued to keep our home up for sale hoping we would be able to sell it and then go over to Hungary to look for another house.

As Christmas drew nearer, we went to a relative's sixtieth birthday party. My husband started to suffer with a flu virus two days beforehand. I was reluctant now to go to the party, as he was not well, but he was determined to go. I thought I would say I had a headache and come away at about 9 pm as I was driving and it was about twenty miles away, this would have been a convenient excuse. Jim seemed to be enjoying himself and appeared to be well as 9 pm approached so I did not attempt to leave that early.

Unfortunately, I found out afterwards that my decision was unwise as one more pint of lager caused him to slur his speech and stagger. Too late, he had shown himself up, and as we left I wondered what his relatives thought about this and felt ashamed.

We went to our daughter's home for dinner on Christmas day and were looking forward to Christmas with our family. My husband was still not well, but this did not stop him from having plenty to drink at the home of our future son-in-law's parents. This was the first time that we had met them. We then went on to our daughter's home. Our eldest daughter's boyfriend had a pulled a muscle in his leg and was limping about so I asked him if he would like me to pray for healing of this injury. He agreed to this. The pain left him and he could move his leg normally again. He was surprised.

I was shocked when a little later my husband, having had quite a lot to drink, decided to turn our two daughters against me. His behaviour had dramatically changed and he became unpleasant and unpredictable. As my daughters had been drinking heavily as well, they both became quite hostile towards me. I felt like leaving at that point but knew that this would probably make the situation worse so gritting my teeth I remained. We eventually had our meal at about 5 pm four hours later than planned!

It was with a huge sigh of relief when I left the 'party.' excusing myself at about 6 pm to check on our dog at home. As I played with him, opened his presents for him and fed him some leftovers from the Christmas dinner I felt a lot more peaceful knowing that I was no longer with my drunken family on this Christmas night. Storm was a lovely dog and appreciated this very much as he had been left on his own for some hours. I rang my daughter to say that I had a headache and did not feel well enough to go back. I enjoyed the evening with Storm sat and watched a comedy on TV and then went to bed.

I looked at the alarm clock as I heard a taxi draw up outside it was 1.30 am and Jim had arrived home.

When I woke up on Boxing Day, I felt rough. It seemed as though I had caught the flu virus. I stayed in bed all day, and felt so bad that I needed to stay in bed for a week. I had no sympathy and very little understanding from my husband and two daughters. This really hurt. I started getting pains in my chest and pins and needles sensations around my heart. I had to rest. I could not eat anything sweet as this was like poison to my body. My husband enjoyed all the Christmas food, but apart from some savoury items, I could not touch it.

I went down with this flu twice more and spent about a week in bed each time over the next month and a half. Eventually I realised that my husband was passing the cough on to me as he had a permanent cough from his smoking, which he chose to ignore, and I was sure that my immune system was very weak by now. I told him that we would have to sleep separately if he wanted to continue smoking, and not go to the doctor to try to sort this out.

About a month later though, he started to feel unwell and needed to spend about a week resting as he now had a chest infection. He had a temperature of over 38°C so I made sure that he had some medication from the chemist and vitamin C in oranges and grapes to aid his recovery. Still he refused to see the doctor.

Almost a week later he started to feel a little better, but although he was comfortable and had newspapers to read and the TV to watch he became so fed up just resting that he decided to go to his friend's house for a drink. When he returned he was quite red in the face. The following day he looked ill at ease and uncomfortable but he did not tell me how he felt until during the evening. Apparently, he had pains in his stomach, a headache and felt shivery. I suggested that he go to bed but he laid down on the settee so I took his temperature, which was 40°C. I should have called the doctor or ambulance, but I decided to look after him myself, as I knew he would have made a big fuss if I had tried to ring for help. I rang NHS Direct in another room and they advised me to start giving him some paracetamol again to bring the temperature down. I slept on the floor close to him and set the alarm clock to check up on him every couple of hours. His temperature started to go down, but as it did, he sweated so badly that he needed his clothes and bedding changing three times, as they were soaked through. The following morning I took him in the car to the doctors. The doctor gave him some penicillin and she told him to go for a chest x ray, after I mentioned my concern about his cough. He pulled a face and the doctor looked at me with distain, as though I was a meddling wife. I thought that is it, if he becomes ill again, I will call an ambulance or the doctor and not try to help him myself. He took the course of penicillin, but the following weekend he went out for a drink again and had another high temperature of 38°C, but this time he recovered more quickly.

He refused to go for the chest x ray and I knew it was no good trying to control him by insisting that he go. I could not help worrying about him though.

As the effects of the penicillin wore off, so did the cough return, and I found myself still having to sleep separately, unless I wanted to have my immune system attacked again suffering regular sore throats, swollen glands in my neck, colds and coughs.

The Al-Anon meetings that I attended helped me to surrender all of this to God and this gave me peace of mind in that I had no control over his behaviour or his decision making as to whether he would help himself or not. Thankfully, Al-Anon meetings are available throughout the world to support families and friends of alcoholics.

A couple of months later my husband received a letter from his doctor to attend the surgery. He went along and the doctor said that he would like him to go for blood tests. Again, he refused to go and then kept promising to go, when I said that I was concerned about his health. I continued to pray about the situation hoping that his health would not deteriorate any further as I feared that he might have liver damage due to the symptoms he was experiencing.

I invited several friends and relatives round for meals, or for the evening, regularly to try to detract my husband from going to see the friend that he drank with about three times a week. Although this helped, he still went to see his friend twice a week. This man was angry with God for the death of his wife. He had recently suffered with a stroke and had no respect for his own health. He continued to drink and smoke heavily and encouraged Jim to do the same. I started to invite more Christian friends and relatives round and we prayed for a change of heart within him. I noticed changes as he became far less confrontational. Perhaps my working on the Al-Anon programme had helped a little.

I started to feel a lot better in myself and felt as though I had more patience and was better able to cope with traumas, when they arose, more calmly.

CHAPTER 12

God's compassion and answer to prayer

My husband and I decided to have a holiday on the coast. We found a beautiful log cabin in woodland close to the sea. As we loved wildlife, it was a peaceful haven for us and Storm our dog who loved going for walks in the woods. We were welcomed with blue skies, sunshine and birds singing. Storm found many grey squirrels to chase and was dismayed when they ran up the tree out of reach. We experienced a relaxing and enjoyable time as we wandered through beautiful coastal fishing villages and came upon a bird sanctuary.

Everything was fine until we had our evening meal at a nearby restaurant. Jim drank so much that it was not long before he was slurring his speech and staggering. It was humiliating as we left and this filled me with anxiety.

The following day I asked Jim if he would like to go to Walsingham, the National Shrine of Mary, Mother of Jesus. We had visited this spiritual place before and I wondered if it might help Jim in some way. As we arrived, the relics of a recent French saint were brought into the Basilica for pilgrims to file past, venerate, and ask for her prayers. I could not believe the timing, as we had arrived just at this momentous time before any crowds descended on the area. We filed past the relics of this amazing saint and I silently asked her to intercede for Jim to stop drinking, as I was concerned about his health. The Basilica filled up and became crowded. We then stayed for a special mass, which was a great blessing.

Sadly, Jim's drinking continued and about four months later during January we met with his sister Joan and his brother-in-law Kevin for an after Christmas lunch, as they were unable to come and see us during Christmas. We enjoyed a nice meal together, but Jim was still drinking a lot. I suspected that Jim was really struggling as his sister had been very unpleasant to him years previously and had never apologised.

When we returned home, he decided to go straight out again to his friend's home who lived near the canal. I was concerned about him in case he became drunk and fell into the canal. He arrived home late that evening very drunk.

The following morning when he got up, he found that he had lost the feeling in his hands and feet. I asked him if he was going to go to the doctors but he refused. The following day, he asked me to drive him to work, as I usually did where he had a part time job in an old people's home. He found a spare stick and shuffled round with the aid of this. He struggled for about two weeks before he finally decided to go to the doctors. I took him in our car. His doctor told him that he was suffering from 'drop foot' as he could not lift his feet properly and was tripping over them. He told him that he must never drink alcohol again and had him admitted into hospital immediately.

When we arrived at the hospital, he received numerous tests including a lumbar puncture. Then admitted on to a ward and put on a drip for a week. The specialist told him that he might be lucky and the nerves that had been damaged in his hands, feet and legs may or may not heal. I was concerned though about his brain, as he did not seem to recognise me as his wife. The hospital supplied him with leg and foot braces to enable him to walk more easily and special aids to enable him to hold a knife, fork and spoon to feed himself. He was given physiotherapy and diagnosed with peripheral neuropathy.

While Jim was in hospital, I went to the large chest freezer in the garage to take out some food for a meal. I was horrified to find lined up on top of the freezer a machete and numerous large knives all laid out. As I gazed upon this upsetting sight, I remembered how I had told Jim how much I hated knives. This seemed to have been done to scare me. I wrapped each one up in padded parcels wrapped in numerous sheets of newspaper and placed them all in the bin with more rubbish on the top. The contents of the bin were due to be collected by the refuge collection lorry the next day.

Knowing that Jim had done this deliberately I got in touch with a counsellor who specialised in alcohol related problems. She told me that when an alcoholic is reaching the final stage of their disease that they can become paranoid and could think that you are a tiger and lash out with a knife. She advised me to leave him and take the dog with me.

I prayed about this and decided to remain at home for the time being. After he had received all the treatment that he needed I collected him from the hospital. When he returned home, he was depressed and moaned a lot. I tried to cheer him up with the TV, newspapers, fishing and metal detecting magazines, but he was really down as he could only walk very slowly now with a walking stick. This meant that he could no longer go and see his alcoholic friend in the village.

Jim had finally reached his 'bottom' and made a decision to go into AA recovery and stop smoking. He had a sponsor and as I had my recovery programme, we were both now in recovery. Sadly this did not mean that everything was fine between us as there were still the 'isms' of dry drunkenness (when he behaved like an alcoholic although he was not drinking), which involved moodiness and me feeling as if I was walking on eggshells. Thankfully, there were many happier times that we spent together and Jim started a new hobby of stick making. He found an excellent tutor to help him with this, joined a stick making club and we went to many events where they were on display.

Slowly he recovered the use of his hands and feet again, but unfortunately, he appeared to have a form of dementia. His memory became very bad, he could not retain information for very long, and he repeatedly asked the same questions. He used to accuse me of not telling him about things when I had.

It was not long before Jim met his friend in the village again because he was now becoming more mobile. He visited him regularly once again, starting to smoke intensely including drugs.

He used to return home with a really bad attitude towards me and stopped going to AA. The drugs that he took appeared to be mind-altering ones. His eyes did not look right because he often stared into space as if he was on a different planet.

After various requests from his doctor, he finally agreed to go for blood tests because the chest infection that he had was not improving. He was sent to the hospital for a scan and it revealed a shadow on his lung. More detailed scans followed, which showed an inoperable tumour. This was devastating news and I really struggled to come to terms with the diagnosis from his specialist. I repeatedly took him to the hospital, which was fifteen miles away for courses of chemotherapy and radiotherapy.

Jim ate well despite the chemotherapy he was undergoing and on one occasion, we went out for a meal with family. His son-in-law foolishly challenged him to a second large meal, a mixed grill, which he ate. On the way home, he had severe pains in his stomach and leg. I took him straight to our local hospital but they sent him home and told me to call an ambulance if the condition got any worse. They gave him some painkillers and the pain subsided.

The following morning the pain at the top of his leg suddenly became unbearable. I had never seen him in such pain before. He wanted me to call an ambulance, which was very unusual for him, so I rang 999 and requested help. Within ten minutes, the paramedics arrived. They examined him, diagnosed a blood clot in his leg and took him straight to hospital in the next city. I followed in the car.

Our eldest daughter left work and came straight to the hospital when she heard that her father was ill. The surgeon took us to one side, told us both that he could lose his leg and he could even lose his life. He explained that he needed to try to remove the blood clot. I had, by now been at the hospital for a number of hours. After Jim went down to the operating theatre, I told Jill that I had to go home and let our dog out and would return as soon as I could. I suggested that we both pray for her father for the operation and his recovery.

Thankfully, soon after I returned to the hospital the surgeon came to see Jill and I and told us that the operation had been successful and that he was recovering. We thanked him very much and we were greatly relieved. I hoped that the answer to prayer would help her to return to the Christian faith that she once had.

Lots of prayer went up for Jim from myself and my friends and he went into remission and led a reasonably normal life apart from meeting up daily with friends in a pub.

Sadly his mental decline continued. Repeatedly he would try to get into a scalding bath because he had put very little or no cold water in with the hot when he ran it off. I had to cool it down and he resented this. His doctor suspected that he may have Korsakoff's Syndrome, but he refused to diagnose him unless he himself asked for help. One day he spent nearly two hours in the bath and refused to get out. I was about to call a doctor or ambulance for help when he managed to get out.

I provided Jim with a good diet to encourage him to eat well, but also made sure that it was healthy food. Sadly, though, he used to go out to the local shop and buy himself large packets of biscuits and sweets to eat which undermined the healthy diet he was eating. He had been warned at the hospital not to have too much sugary food.

It was a terrible shock when about six months later during his check up at the hospital,, the specialist told Jim that there was nothing more that he could do to help him.

After this, he just went to pieces. He gave up and became very depressed. He went to stay at our daughter and son-in-law's for a few days leaving me on my own lonely and very sad.

Soon after this, our dog was mysteriously taken ill with repeated vomiting and sadly did not recover. I took him to the vets and he stayed in their hospital for several days while they carried out tests on him. They told me that he had kidney failure and there was nothing they could do to help him. This broke my heart, to be parted from my loyal friend who had been there for me in all the difficulties I was experiencing. I was convinced that my husband had poisoned the dog and that I could be next.

As my husband steadily deteriorated, I found a dementia support group who were very helpful and supportive and of course, I still had my Al-Anon meeting.

One day, quite unexpectedly Jim turned to me and said that he was sorry.

Jim declined severely and I could not leave him. His doctor had him admitted into hospital with a high temperature and pains in his neck and shoulder where the cancer had spread. He recovered from the high temperature, but was very confused and the nurse said that his confusion was dementia. He did not know where he was or what day it was. I requested help at home and a special hospital bed was supplied, a commode, hospice nurses twice a day and three nights a week and the district nurse to call out as well. This support was invaluable.

Our two daughters came round to see if they could help. Jim's sister and brother-in-law also turned up to see him. He was very weak and frail by this time, but nothing could have prepared me for the way my daughters spoke to me in front of Joan and Kevin accusing me of being rough with their very sick father, who by this time needed 24/7 care from me. The accusations were completely unjustified and I do not know where they came from. I was very upset about this and wondered what further figments of his imagination had twisted things around before he spoke to his daughters. By now, the nurses were coming in twice a day and overnight for three nights a week. When I stayed up to be with him, our daughters stayed up as well. The hospice nurse suggested that we take it in turns in shifts so that each of us could rest but they refused to do that. The nurse was dismayed at their bad attitude.

Sadly, his GP, did not support my children or myself, by explaining that Jim may have Korsakoff's Syndrome, and through the misunderstandings of this insidious illness, our daughters took everything that he said at face value. Through the lies and stories that he had made up our daughters believed him and turned more and more against me. All this heartache on top of everything else could have been avoided if everything had been explained clearly to us all.

Before their father was taken into hospital for the last time the District Nurse came out and said as she examined him that he had dementia because of the way he was talking.

Several days later, his temperature shot up again and he was becoming very dehydrated, as he did not want to drink. A doctor came out and had him admitted to hospital. This time when we arrived there, we were told we could stay with him in a side ward and we were able to sleep there as well. The hospital staff were very kind and caring, but despite this, Jill and Kate accused two male nurses who had to turn him and lift him while they changed the sheets on his bed of being rough. I felt ashamed of my daughters for their very out of order attitude.

Later that evening as he was starting to fade away our daughters gave him alcohol to drink in defiance. This was unwise, as he had just spent time on a drip to rehydrate him. My youngest daughter returned home, as she did not want to see her father die. I sat up all night, held his hand, and prayed for him and at about 7 am he breathed his last. I managed to wake and call Jill as he faded away. He had refused to see the priest before he died so I asked him to come and pray for him now. I took Jill home and returned to my home, which seemed very empty.

I met up with my daughters to arrange to go and organise the funeral. As it was getting close to Christmas, I hoped that the funeral could be held prior to Christmas. We went to the funeral directors and spent about two and a half hours there as my two daughters insisted that their father was cremated, and placed in his family's grave, in the next City. I wanted to buy a double grave for him and myself and have him buried locally so that I could go and take flowers regularly but my two daughters were very awkward and as a result of messing the funeral directors about the price rose by a further thousand pounds. Eventually I insisted on my request and everything was arranged for the funeral.

My daughters paid me a visit to collect photographs of their father. They brought my grandson and granddaughter with them. They insisted on taking all of my photograph albums and stacked them up to take with them. Their attitude was menacing. The way they were behaving, they appeared to be high on drugs. I asked them to leave the albums with me and choose the photographs they wanted of their father but they were insistent and when I tried to stop them, they confronted me with physical abuse. I called the police and they fled. I was in a terrible state by now and shook from head to foot. The police called and were very sympathetic and promised to call on both of them to talk to them. They suggested that if they ever came back to see me again it should be one at a time and that I was to have a friend with me. I felt devastated, I had lost my husband, and my daughters had turned against me and of course now I was left without my loyal friend, Storm my dog. The mourning for my husband ceased at that point and I froze in horror.

A friend came round to see me and brought a beautiful plant. This cheered me up. I found the support of my friends, my Al-Anon friends and friends at the dementia support group kept me going, but could still not grieve because of the terrible shock that I had received. As if this was not enough my daughters would not have anything to do with me and at the funeral, they tried to play a CD, which was completely inappropriate and condemned a fisherman's wife. This was another way of having a go at me, but thankfully, the CD would not work.

The priest did not use the information I had asked him to commemorate Jim's life, especially during the happier times, instead he preached the good news to a full church of many people who were unsaved. Thankfully, a few of my friends attended the funeral and were there for me afterwards.

I now had a lonely life with no family and I was devastated that I could not see my grandchildren. Most of my friends were married and were busy at the weekends when I felt the most lonely. Thankfully, my Saviour Jesus continued to carry me through this dark time of my life.

About five months later, I reached a point where I felt that something needed to change. I felt I had reached a crossroads and was not sure whether go into a convent to live or to meet someone else. I thought and prayed about it a lot because I was so lonely.

I casually looked on a Christian internet site and decided to join it to find a friend. It wasn't long before I met David who was quite good looking. He was involved in his church but also had his own local radio show. After I had given him permission, he rang me every evening. A couple of months later we met up when I went to stay at a nearby pilgrimage site. He treated me very well, taking me to his church, introducing me to all his friends and then out for a lovely meal. While I was in the area, he also took me to a charming seaside village. The location and the friendship seemed idyllic.

We continued to see each other and became closer. I helped him with a special church service he was leading and I enjoyed being with someone, whose faith also meant so much to him.

We remained close for another year and during this time my daughters still had very little to do with me. I was only able to see them to give them or my grandchildren birthday or Christmas presents. Then quite unexpectedly, David proposed to me. I accepted and he bought me a beautiful engagement ring. I decided to go and live nearer to him as he lived in a picturesque part of the country. Before I could sell my bungalow there was some work to be done. The large garden needed to be tidied and the hedges cut. There was the loft to empty and the garage to clear. When all this work was done

I was able to place it on the market. It sold for a good price within a week. I couldn't believe it.

David and I searched for a similar bungalow for me close to where he lived but on the first attempt nothing suitable was found. The next time we looked for properties there was very little choice as it was Christmas time. Out of three properties, that we looked at there was one which seemed to be ideal. It was in a nice quiet location with a lovely walled garden easy to maintain. It had a large kitchen/diner a comfortable lounge and three bedrooms. I put in an offer and it was accepted. I felt exhilarated. I spent a lovely Christmas with David. We went to a candle lit midnight service on Christmas Eve and out for an enjoyable Christmas dinner on Christmas Day. We travelled to the coast another day and spoke about our plans as we walked across the beach. The waves chased David as he got too close to the sea. I felt very happy and returned to start sorting out my home. I knew that I needed to downsize so I sold furniture and set myself a goal to clear the loft in a week, which was quite a big task, but also the garage in a week, which was even worse! The charity shop I chose to take many items that I could no longer keep became well stocked up. First of all, though I gave family heirlooms and items of value to my children.

Soon my home was sorted. All the packing was done and a date set for the move. I arranged to meet up with friends before I left.

Two months later in my new home, I had, with David's help bought some new curtains and furniture for a bungalow with a completely different layout to the one that I had left.

We enjoyed many months of happy times together.

Slowly our relationship started to deteriorate. I found that the person that I thought I knew was no longer the same person. He cared for his elderly mother and I had been happy to help him with this. Now her health declined further with confusion and dementia setting in. It became difficult to leave her on her own. David was adamant that she was not going to be put into a home and I remained happy to support him in this. Unfortunately the carers who came in twice a day to her home were unreliable and some of them unhelpful. This grieved David and when he discussed it with me, I tried to make helpful suggestions how to sort the problems out. He ignored these suggestions and continued to moan about the situation. He dropped going to church and the special service that he had led and put all his efforts into his radio show. This upset me as I felt that he could have found private carers to come in perhaps about once or twice a week for a couple of hours so that we could have some time together on our own. Not only did he refuse this he also went into moods that lasted for several days. I discovered that at these times I could not reason with him or discuss anything with him. This I could not handle at all because this was how my father had treated my mother and myself all those years ago when I was a child. I discovered that the family disease of alcoholism had affected his grandparents and parents. His sister was very unpleasant and bossy ordering him and his mother about. By the following Christmas, I was ready to finish with David as I felt near a nervous breakdown. Soon after Christmas, I finished with him.

I was happy to remain in my bungalow, as my daughters were still distant towards me. I made a life for myself in this city where I had settled down and felt comfortable here. I was asked at my local church if I would play the organ for them on Sunday mornings. I was a little nervous about this, as I had not done it before. In time, I started to really enjoy this work, as I planned the music for several weeks in advance enabling me to practise it. I also went to a church in the centre of the city to enquire if anything was being done to help homeless people. I must have called just at the right time, as I was then invited to join a training day, for people from the church to go out and pray for those on the streets. I enthusiastically agreed and turned up the following Saturday as arranged. The course was very down to earth. It was basically training us to understand that Jesus went out and prayed for people and we were to go out in His Name and pray as we felt led by the Holy Spirit.

After the day's training, we were split into pairs and asked to go out and pray for anyone we felt led to approach. I teamed up with another lady and we prayed for several people who were glad to be asked if they needed prayer, which was really encouraging. After that I went along every week to join the ecumenical team for prayers and then to go out on to the street and pray for people in Jesus's Name. On one occasion, there was snow on the ground and Paul and I approached a homeless man who looked very thin and pale. I asked him if he would like some prayer and he immediately said yes. We prayed for him and then I urged him to go to the church that we had come from as they had a homeless helper there. The Lord had given me a heart for the homeless.

The following week when I went along, I was told that the young man had stopped taking heroin and alcohol and gone to the church. The team there had prayed for him and when one of them looked round afterwards they saw the young man kneeling at the altar, and breaking down in tears. He had received a remarkable healing and we all praised God.

I remained in the city for another year before I felt that God was urging me to move back closer to my daughter and grandchildren. My other daughter had moved away with her work. There seemed to be a glimmer of hope now, as my daughter and grandchildren came to see me for a few days and we spent some happy times at the coast.

I did some decorating, smartened the place up and then put the property on the market for sale. It took several months before anyone put in an offer, which was accepted. Unfortunately, it was not a genuine offer and two months later fell through. I was devastated and had to put the bungalow back on to the market again. Eventually one of the original people who viewed it managed to sell her property and put in an offer for mine. This accepted, I then went as soon as I could to my hometown to view two bungalows. It was winter and there was snow on the ground and more promised. I was unsure if I was doing the right thing. The temperature outside was minus six degrees centigrade. I loaded up the car and set off. When I got to the ring road, it was clear. Two and a half hours later, I arrived at my destination and as I was approaching, a blizzard struck. I could scarcely see in front of me as I drove along the village road on the outskirts. I managed to find somewhere to have a meal before viewing the three properties that I had arranged with the estate agent a few days before. I discovered that the property I was most interested in, had been sold! I went to look at a similar one, which needed more work doing to it. After looking round this property, it was not long before I felt that this was the one to put in an offer for. My first offer was a little lower than the asking price and was refused, but the second offer, which still saved me money, was accepted. I was ecstatic and went to the nearby convent to stay the night, wondering if I was doing the right thing with the weather conditions as they were. It blew a gale all night. I hardly dare look out of the window in the morning, but amazingly, I discovered that there was just a light sprinkling of snow. Saying goodbye to my friends as the convent I started the car up and discovered that the temperature was still minus six centigrade. I went to mass at the local church and viewed the bungalow for the second time. Starting to drive home before leaving I felt God was urging me to go and have a hot meal first.

Afterwards I was glad that I had listened to what the Almighty was showing me. I had a good journey until I reached halfway then there was a sudden snowstorm, which was so intense that visibility was virtually nil. I was on a motorway and slowed down according to the weather conditions. Then the sun came out and further along an equally intense snowstorm. My windscreen was icing over on the outside despite the warm air from the heating in the car directed at it. As I started to approach the city, I saw numerous abandoned cars, an accident with a lorry and a car and there was snow on the motorway. I saw a snowplough clearing snow on the road. I continued driving gingerly, praying as I went and arrived back in a familiar area. As I drove along the ring road, I noticed that the road that I would normally use was impassable! I drove along a similar road further up expecting to have to abandon my car at any time. God blessed my journey so much that I arrived safely at my home and was even able to put the car away in the garage. I was so thankful and amazed. On the news that evening, I discovered that the roads that I had travelled on were very dangerous that morning with people abandoning cars everywhere and bad driving conditions during the rush hour. By having the meal before I set off, I avoided all these problems. What a blessing.

Three months later, I was able to move into my new home, close to my daughter and grandchildren.

Six months after this, God gave me an opportunity to talk to my youngest daughter and two grandchildren. I explained to them how my husband, after he had been drinking, regularly became very unpleasant and started shouting at me saying many nasty things to make me react. Eventually, I did react and may have said something unpleasant, he, then, seizing the opportunity, wrote down what I had said and showed it to both of my daughters and his friends to turn them against me. I explained that he had done this repeatedly and, also he had told lies because his friend had accused me of being a witch twice which really upset me as nothing could be further from the truth as I am a Christian and serve Jesus not the devil. They listened and understood and after that, my daughter couldn't have been nicer towards me. She invited me to her home to spend Christmas with her and my grandchildren – something I had longed for over many years. Several days later, I was able to speak to my eldest daughter about this to. As she was closest to her father, I thought that this was going to be difficult, but when I spoke to her, it felt as though they were not my words but the Lord speaking through me and thankfully, she responded in a similar way to her sister. It was lovely to see her when she visited me. It was a moving and emotional time. I cannot thank the Heavenly Father enough after many years of prayer for giving me my family back again.

Witchcraft is not confined to fairy tales but sadly is alive and active in this country. Witches curse family members and others around them and in cases where people do not know Jesus, the enemy walks into their lives. This is the enemy's plan. Witchcraft is spiritual bullying carried out by cowards.

God has given us free will and stands by patiently waiting for this country to come back to Him, and to recognise afresh that His dear Son Jesus died to save us from our sins.

Nine years after my father died and after a considerable amount of prayer to eliminate the witchcraft that he practised, I felt led to go and speak to Father John about deliverance healing as I was not sure whether all the prayers necessary had been completed. He told me that the mass was so powerful that I could confidently take my prayer intentions to mass and expect answer to prayer. He also told me how he finds Mary's intercession very powerful especially in protection. Armed with this knowledge I started to take my prayers to mass to pray for healing and sure enough found this was a powerful tool in healing ministry. I felt more secure in praying this way as so many times before I had received deliverance healing only to find that it was incomplete leaving behind doubts and fears.